SERIES ENDORSEMENTS

"There are so many fine commentaries available today, but it's great to have a reliable author you can turn to for solid Reformed reflection on Scripture. In this case, there are sixteen of them—friends and fellow shepherds who have given me great insight into God's Word over the years. I'm looking forward eagerly to Fesko's Galatians commentary—and to each one after that!"

Michael S. Horton

J. Gresham Machen Professor of
Apologetics and Systematic Theology at
Westminster Seminary California

Host of the *White Horse Inn* Talk Show

Editor-in-Chief of *Modern Reformation* magazine

"Those of us who have promoted and practiced *lectio continua* expository preaching through the years eagerly await the volumes Tolle Lege Press has announced in its *Lectio Continua Expository Commentary on the New Testament*. We are equally eager to read such a series written by pastors who have practiced the method in their churches. The international and interdenominational character of the series will only add to the richness of its insights."

T. David Gordon

Professor of Religion and Greek at Grove City College

Author of *Why Johnny Can't Preach* (P&R, 2009)

SERIES ENDORSEMENTS

"As the history of preaching is unfolded, it becomes clear how important the orderly, systematic preaching through the Scriptures has been, and why it has been a favorite homiletic approach over the centuries. One is surprised to discover how many of history's great preachers made a regular practice of preaching through one book of the Bible after another. Origen, the first Christian preacher from whom we have any sizable collection of sermons, preached most of his sermons on the *lectio continua*. We find the same with John Chrysostom who is usually referred to as the greatest Christian preacher. We find the same true of Augustine as well. At the time of the Protestant Reformation, Zwingli, Calvin, Bucer, and Knox followed this system regularly, and they passed it on to the Puritans. Today, we see a real revival of *lectio continua* preaching. *The Lectio Continua Expository Commentary on the New Testament* represents a wonderful opportunity for the Church to recover a truly expository pulpit."

Hughes Oliphant Old

John H. Leith Professor of Reformed Theology and Worship at Erskine Theological Seminary
Author of *The Reading and Preaching of the Scriptures in the Worship of the Christian Church* (7 vols., Eerdmans, 2007)

"The concept behind this series is a fascinating one and, given the list of authors, I am confident that the final product will not disappoint. This promises to be a great resource for churches seeking to know the word of God more fully."

Carl R. Trueman

Professor of Church History at
Westminster Theological Seminary in Philadelphia, PA

FORTHCOMING VOLUMES IN THE
LECTIO CONTINUA SERIES:

First and Second Thessalonians
Daniel R. Hyde

The Gospel of John
Terry L. Johnson

First Peter
Jon D. Payne

First Corinthians
Kim Riddlebarger

THE LECTIO CONTINUA

EXPOSITORY COMMENTARY ON THE NEW TESTAMENT

Galatians

J. V. Fesko

Series Editor
Jon D. Payne

TOLLE LEGE PRESS
POWDER SPRINGS, GEORGIA

The Lectio Continua Expository Commentary Series

Galatians
by J. V. Fesko

Series Editor: Jon D. Payne

Produced and Distributed by:

TOLLE LEGE PRESS
3150-A Florence Road
Powder Springs, GA 30127

www.TolleLegePress.com
800-651-0211

Cover design by Jennifer Tyson

Typeset by Luis Lovelace

Photograph of Grossmünster Cathedral by Pedro Szekely:
http://www.flickr.com/people/pedrosz/. Used with permission.

ISBN: 978-0-9831457-7-6

Consulting Editors

DR. JOEL R. BEEKE (Ph.D. Westminster Seminary)
Professor of Systematic Theology and Homiletics and President of
Puritan Reformed Theological Seminary
Pastor of the Heritage Netherlands Reformed Congregation
Editorial Director of Reformation Heritage Books,
Grand Rapids, Michigan

DR. T. DAVID GORDON (Ph.D. Union Theological Seminary)
Professor of Religion and Greek at Grove City College, Pennsylvania
Former Associate Professor of New Testament at
Gordon-Conwell Theological Seminary, Boston, Massachusetts

DR. DAVID W. HALL (Ph.D. Whitefield Seminary)
Pastor of Midway Presbyterian Church (PCA) in
Powder Springs, Georgia
General Editor of and contributor to *The Calvin 500 Series* (P&R)

REV. ERIC LANDRY (M.Div. Westminster Seminary California)
Pastor of Christ Presbyterian Church in Murrieta, California
Executive Editor of *Modern Reformation* magazine

DR. MALCOLM MACLEAN (D.Min. Highland Theological College)
Pastor of Greyfriars Free Church of Scotland in Inverness
Editor of Christian Focus Publication's Mentor imprint

DR. WILLIAM M. SCHWEITZER (Ph.D. University of Edinburgh)
Pastor of Gateshead Presbyterian Church (EPCEW) in
Newcastle/Gateshead, England

DR. GUY P. WATERS (Ph.D. Duke University)
Professor of New Testament at Reformed Theological Seminary
Former Assistant Professor of Biblical Studies at
Belhaven College, Jackson, Mississippi

Dedicated to
JACK AND LOGAN FESKO

Contents

ABBREVIATIONS USED IN THE LECTIO CONTINUA SERIES

*	Author's translation
ca.	Circa
CNTC	Calvin's New Testament Commentaries
CTS	Calvin Translation Society
ESV	English Standard Version
KJV	King James Version
LXX	Septuagint
Macc.	Maccabees—Apocryphal Book
NICNT	New International Commentary on the New Testament
NICOT	New International Commentary on the Old Testament
NIV	New International Version
NKJ	New King James
NRSV	New Revised Standard Version
NSBT	New Studies in Biblical Theology
WCF	Westminster Confession of Faith
WSC	Westminster Shorter Catechism
ZECNT	Zondervan Exegetical Commentary on the New Testament

BOOKS OF THE BIBLE

Genesis	Gen.	2 Chronicles	2 Chron.	Daniel	Dan.
Exodus	Exod.	Ezra	Ezra	Hosea	Hos.
Leviticus	Lev.	Nehemiah	Neh.	Joel	Joel
Numbers	Num.	Esther	Esth.	Amos	Amos
Deuteronomy	Deut.	Job	Job	Obadiah	Obad.
Joshua	Josh.	Psalms	Ps.	Jonah	Jonah
Judges	Judg.	Proverbs	Prov.	Micah	Mic.
Ruth	Ruth	Ecclesiastes	Eccl.	Nahum	Nah.
1 Samuel	1 Sam.	Song of Solomon	Song	Habakkuk	Hab.
2 Samuel	2 Sam.	Isaiah	Isa.	Zephaniah	Zeph.
1 Kings	1 Kings	Jeremiah	Jer.	Haggai	Hag.
2 Kings	2 Kings	Lamentations	Lam.	Zechariah	Zech.
1 Chronicles	1 Chron.	Ezekiel	Ezek.	Malachi	Mal.

Matthew	Matt.	Ephesians	Eph.	Hebrews	Heb.
Mark	Mark	Philippians	Phil.	James	James
Luke	Luke	Colossians	Col.	1 Peter	1 Pet.
John	John	1 Thessalonians	1 Thess.	2 Peter	2 Pet.
Acts	Acts	2 Thessalonians	2 Thess.	1 John	1 John
Romans	Rom.	1 Timothy	1 Tim.	2 John	2 John
1 Corinthians	1 Cor.	2 Timothy	2 Tim.	3 John	3 John
2 Corinthians	2 Cor.	Titus	Titus	Jude	Jude
Galatians	Gal.	Philemon	Philem.	Revelation	Rev.

The Grossmünster Cathedral in Zurich, Switzerland where Huldrych Zwingli preached from 1519–1531

Series Introduction

The greatest need of the church today is the recovery of sound biblical preaching that faithfully explains and applies the text, courageously confronts sin, and boldly trumpets forth the sovereign majesty, law, and promises of God. This type of powerful preaching has vanished in many quarters of the evangelical church only to be replaced by that which is anemic and man-centered. Instead of doctrinally rich exposition which strengthens faith and fosters Christian maturity, the standard fare has become informal, chatty, anecdote-laden messages, leaving unbelievers confused, and believers in a state of chronic spiritual adolescence.[1]

There is indeed a dire need for the recovery of solid biblical preaching. Not only does reformation of this sort lead Christ's sheep back to the verdant pastures of His soul-nourishing Word, it also provides a good example to future generations of ministers. For this reason, I am pleased to introduce *The Lectio Continua Expository Commentary on the New Testament* (LCECNT), a new series of expository commentaries authored by an array of seasoned pastor-scholars from various Reformed denominations on both sides of the Atlantic.

---

1. A stinging, yet constructive critique of modern-day preaching is found in T. David Gordon's *Why Johnny Can't Preach: The Media Have Shaped the Messengers* (Phillipsburg, NJ: P&R, 2009). "I have come to recognize that many, many individuals today have never been under a steady diet of competent preaching. . . . As starving children in Manila sift through the landfill for food, Christians in many churches today have never experienced genuine soul-nourishing preaching, and so they just pick away at what is available to them, trying to find a morsel of spiritual sustenance or helpful counsel here or there" (Gordon, *Why Johnny Can't Preach*, 17).

What is the *lectio continua* method of preaching? It is simply the uninterrupted, systematic, expository proclamation of God's Word— verse by verse, chapter by chapter, book by book. It is a system, unlike topical or thematic preaching, that endeavors to deliver the whole counsel of God (Acts 20:26–27). Christian discipleship is impoverished when large portions of Scripture are ignored. Carried out faithfully, the *lectio continua* method ensures that every passage is mined for its riches (even those verses which are obscure, controversial, or hard to swallow). Paul states that "all Scripture is breathed out by God and profitable for teaching, for reproof, for correction, and for training in righteousness, that the man of God may be competent, equipped for every good work" (2 Tim. 3:16–17).

Lectio continua preaching has a splendid heritage. It finds its roots in the early church and patristic eras. Its use, however, was revived and greatly expanded during the sixteenth-century Protestant Reformation. When Huldrych Zwingli (d. 1531) arrived at the Zurich Grossmünster in 1519, it was his desire to dispense with the standard lectionary and introduce *lectio continua* preaching to his congregation by moving systematically through the Gospel of Matthew. At first, some members of his church council were suspicious. They were uncomfortable replacing the lectionary with this seemingly new approach. But Zwingli explained that the *lectio continua* method of preaching was not new at all. On the contrary, important figures such as Augustine (d. 430), Chrysostom (d. 407) and Bernard of Clairvaux (d. 1153) all employed this homiletical strategy. Zwingli is quoted by his successor Heinrich Bullinger (d. 1575) as saying that "no friend of evangelical truth could have any reason to complain" about such a method.[2]

---

2. It is interesting to note that, the year before Zwingli began preaching sequentially through books of the Bible, he had received a new edition of Chrysostom's *lectio continua* sermons on Matthew's Gospel. See Hughes Oliphant Old, *The Patristic Roots of Reformed Worship* (Black Mountain, NC: Worship

Series Introduction

Zwingli rightly believed that the quickest way to restore biblical Christianity to the church was to preach the whole counsel of God verse by verse, chapter by chapter, book by book, Lord's Day after Lord's Day, year after year. Other reformers agreed and followed his pattern. In the city of Strasbourg, just ninety miles north of Zurich, men such as Martin Bucer (d. 1551), Wolfgang Capito (d. 1570), and Kaspar Hedio (d. 1552) practiced *lectio continua* preaching. Johannes Oecolampadius (d. 1531) boldly preached the *lectio continua* in Basel. And let us not forget John Calvin (d. 1564); between 1549 and 1564, the Genevan reformer preached sequentially through no fewer than twenty-five books of the Bible (over 2,000 sermons).[3]

The example of these reformers has been emulated by preachers throughout the centuries, from the Post-Reformation age down to the present. In the last half of the twentieth century, Martyn Lloyd-Jones (d. 1981), William Still (d. 1997), James Montgomery Boice (d. 2000), and John MacArthur all boldly marched straight through books of the Bible from their pulpits. But why? Surely we have acquired better, more contemporary methods of preaching? Is the *lectio continua* relevant in our twenty-first century context? In a day when biblical preaching is being increasingly undermined and marginalized by media/story/therapy/personality-driven sermons, even among the avowedly Reformed, these are important questions to consider.

Shortly before the Apostle Paul was martyred in Rome by Emperor Nero, he penned a second epistle to Timothy. In what proved to be some of his final words to his young disciple, he

Press, 2004), 195. Cf. Old's *The Reading and Preaching of the Scriptures in the Worship of the Christian Church,* vol. 4: *The Age of the Reformation* (Grand Rapids, MI: Eerdmans, 2002), and Timothy George, *Reading Scripture with the Reformers* (Downers Grove, IL: IVP Academic, 2011), 228–253. Elements of this introduction are adapted from Jon D. Payne, "The Roaring of Christ through *Lectio Continua* Preaching," *Modern Reformation* (Nov./Dec. 2010; Vol. 19, No. 6): 23–24, and are used by permission of the publisher.

3. T. H. L. Parker, *Calvin's Preaching* (Edinburgh: T&T Clark, 1992), 159.

wrote, "I charge you in the presence of God and of Christ Jesus
... *preach the word*; be ready in season and out of season; reprove,
rebuke, and exhort, with complete patience and teaching" (2
Tim. 4:1–2). This directive was not meant for only Timothy. No,
it is the primary duty of every Christian minister (and church)
to carefully heed and obey these timeless words; according to
God's divine blueprint for ministry, it is chiefly through the
faithful proclamation of the Word that Christ saves, sanctifies,
and comforts the beloved Church for which He died.[4] In other
words, the preaching of the Gospel and the right administration
of the sacraments are the divinely sanctioned and efficacious
means by which Christ and all His benefits of redemption are
communicated to the elect. For this reason alone the *lectio continua* method of preaching should be the predominant, regular
practice of our churches, providing a steady diet of Law and
Gospel from the entirety of God's Word.

Some may ask, "Why another expository commentary series?" First, because in every generation it is highly valuable
to provide fresh, doctrinally sound, and reliable expositions
of God's Word. Every age possesses its own set of theological,
ecclesiastical, and cultural challenges. In addition, it is beneficial for both current and rising ministers in every generation to
have trustworthy contemporary models of biblical preaching.
Second, the LCECNT uniquely features the expositions of an
array of pastors from a variety of Reformed and confessional
traditions. Consequently, this series brings a wealth of exegetical, confessional, cultural, and practical insight, and furnishes
the reader with an instructive and stimulating selection of *lectio
continua* sermons.

This series is not meant to be an academic or highly technical
commentary. There are many helpful exegetical commentaries

---

4. See Matthew 28:18–20; Romans 10:14–17; 1 Corinthians 1:18–21; 1 Peter 1:22–25, 2:2–3; Westminster Shorter Catechism Q. 89.

Series Introduction

written for that purpose. Rather, the aim is to provide *lectio continua* sermons, originally delivered to Reformed congregations, which clearly and faithfully communicate the context, meaning, gravity, and application of God's inerrant Word. Each volume of expositions aspires to be redemptive-historical, covenantal, Reformed and confessional, trinitarian, person-and-work-of-Christ-centered, and teeming with practical application. Therefore, the series will be a profound blessing to every Christian believer who longs to "grow in the grace and knowledge of our Lord and Savior Jesus Christ" (2 Pet. 3:18).

A project of this magnitude does not happen without the significant contributions of many people. First, I want to thank Raymond, Brandon, and Jared Vallorani of Tolle Lege Press. Their willingness to publish this voluminous set of commentaries is less about their desire to blossom as a Reformed publishing house and more about their sincere love for Christ and the faithful proclamation of the Bible. Also, many thanks to my fellow preachers who graciously agreed to participate in this series. It is a privilege to labor with you for the sake of the Gospel, the health and extension of the church, and the recovery of *lectio continua* preaching. Thanks are also due to the editorial staff of Tolle Lege Press, especially Eric Rauch, Vice President of Publishing and Michael Minkoff, Director of Publishing. I would also like to thank Jennifer Tyson for using her exceptional talents in graphic design, Luis Lovelace for his skillful typesetting, and Ross Hodges, Dr. William Schweitzer, Dr. Todd Weaver, Mr. Martin Driggers, Julie Shields, and Rev. Clif Daniell for helping out in the final stages of the editorial process for this first volume.

Thanks also must be given to the elders and congregation of Grace Presbyterian Church, Douglasville, Georgia, for warmly encouraging their minister to work on this time-consuming, yet beneficial, undertaking. Furthermore, I would like to express the deepest gratitude to my dear wife, Marla, and our two precious children, Mary Hannah and Hans. The peace and joy in our home, nurtured by delightful Lord's Days, regular family worship, and a loving, patient wife, makes editing a series like this one possible.

Finally, and most importantly, sincere thanks and praise must be given to our blessed triune God, the eternal fountain of all grace and truth. By his sovereign love and mercy, through faith in the crucified, resurrected, and ascended Christ, we have been "born again, not of perishable seed but of imperishable, through the living and abiding word of God; for 'All flesh is like grass and all its glory like the flower of grass. The grass withers and the flower falls, but the word of the Lord remains forever.' And this word is the good news *that was preached to you*" (1 Pet. 1:23–25).

Jon D. Payne
Series Editor

Preface

This book aims to fulfill the goals of *The Lectio Continua Expository Commentary on the New Testament*. The chief goals of the series are to be rigorously exegetical, God-centered, redemptive-historical, sin-exposing, Gospel-trumpeting, and teeming with application. I have sought to meet these goals, though I have left much of the exegetical nuts-and-bolts behind the scenes, as this series is primarily expositional. At times, I do make reference to some key Greek terminology. In a few places I have modified the English Standard Version, indicated by an asterisk (*) after the text citation. My division of Galatians reflects the original manner in which I preached my sermon series at Geneva Orthodox Presbyterian Church. Exegetically, it may be more advantageous to subdivide the text in a different manner, but sometimes the exigencies of preaching dictate a different course of action.

I have sought to highlight the central importance of the many Old Testament references Paul employs in Galatians. Sadly, far too many in the church are woefully ignorant of the Old Testament, but for Paul, the Old Testament was his Bible—he knew it well. Hence, I emphasized a number of key passages that routinely surface. One theme that Paul regularly employs, for example, is the Exodus. Looking back in the Old Testament to see what hermeneutical effect the advent of Christ had upon Paul's pre- and post-conversion theology should promote a deeper appreciation of the redemptive-historical character of Paul's letter.

After the exposition of each section, I offer theological reflections. These reflections are not intended to be comprehensive but rather helpful observations that grow organically from the text—opportunities to consider how we can apply Paul's message. Keep in mind, though, that application can mean different things to different people. I understand the term to mean that we must seek to carry out the implicit or explicit imperatives of the text, whether corporately or individually. This means that sometimes the application of a text is simple—believe in the Lord Jesus Christ. I have strived to keep applications in concert with the overall thrust of the specific text in question.

There are several illustrations throughout the work. I hope they prove helpful to the reader. Footnotes are sprinkled here and there, but not in such a manner as to make them obtrusive. Likewise, I have offered quotations from Luther, Calvin, Perkins, and Machen. Following C. S. Lewis's advice, it is good to have the breeze of past centuries refreshing one's mind while reading Paul's letter.

I am grateful for the opportunity to contribute to the LCECNT. It is an honor and privilege to participate; I am thankful to Jon Payne and to Tolle Lege Press. I am also thankful to Chris Stevens who carefully read through an early draft of the manuscript and offered helpful corrections and comments. I am especially grateful to my wife, Anneke. She has always been and continues to be supportive of my writing. Val and Rob, thank you for your willingness to let Daddy get some work done instead of playing trains all the time.

I dedicate this book to my nephews, Jack and Logan Fesko. I pray that you will embrace the wonderful gospel of Jesus Christ by God's grace alone by faith alone in Christ alone. I pray that

Preface

you will know what it means to stand justified in the presence of our holy covenant Lord and call on him as Abba Father, no longer knowing him as judge.

J. V. Fesko
January, 2012
Escondido, California

Introduction

The apostle Paul is perhaps one of the more famous figures in antiquity. He once persecuted the church and then, without much explanation, began to promote the very faith he once sought to destroy. Paul went on to write the lion's share of the New Testament, if one measures his contribution by numbers of books rather than numbers of pages. While Paul's epistle to the Romans is perhaps his best-known book, a close second, or perhaps arguably even better known, is his letter to the Galatian churches. Paul's letter was written some time in the late forties or early fifties of the first century and was one of the first books of the New Testament to be written.

Galatians is perhaps best-known for Paul's fiery defense of the gospel. Paul was greatly alarmed at how quickly the Galatian churches had departed from the gospel. He was desperate to pull them back from the edge of apostasy. What was the main problem at Galatia? There was a group of false teachers who had descended upon the Galatian churches and taught them a different gospel. They taught that a person could be justified and saved if he believed in Jesus *and* was circumcised. Paul goes to great lengths to demonstrate the gravity of this error. For this reason, the chief subject of this epistle is, as John Calvin notes, "the justification of man."[1] But what does it mean to be justified?

Stated simply, to be justified is to be declared righteous before the tribunal of God. Justification does not involve a moral transformation of the sinner but only a change of the

---

1. John Calvin, *Galatians, Ephesians, Philippians, and Colossians*, CNTC, eds. David W. Torrance and T. F. Torrance, trans. T. H. L. Parker (Grand Rapids, MI: Eerdmans, [1965] 1999), 4.

GALATIANS

person's legal status. By contrast, sanctification is the sinner's moral and spiritual transformation and gradual conformation to the image of Christ. Sanctification is a process that brings about the transformation of the sinner. Paul argues throughout his epistle that a person is justified by God's grace alone by faith alone in Christ alone. And though justification is but one part of our redemption, it is nevertheless essential as the anchor of salvation.

In our justification by faith alone God imputes (or credits) the perfect law-keeping (or obedience) of Jesus to sinners and transfers the sinner's guilt and penalty for his violation of the law to Christ. There is no amount of effort on the part of sinful man—no amount of obedience—that can secure our justification. Hence, a person is justified by faith alone—we do not contribute our good works. This is why justification is by God's grace alone; God takes the initiative in salvation, not man. Moreover, this is why justification, and ultimately salvation, is by Christ alone. Jesus is the one who saves us. Our salvation is not a joint venture between us and Christ. Paul relentlessly hammers out these truths in his epistle to the Galatians. Though Paul addresses justification by faith alone in great detail, it is not the sole subject of this epistle.

Among the other subjects that Paul unfolds is the doctrine of sanctification. For example, there are a number of places where Paul discusses the importance of "faith working through love" (Gal. 5:6) as it is made manifest by the fruit of the Spirit (Gal. 5:22–23) in the life of the church (Gal. 6:1–10). For Paul, the justified Christian can and should be identified and known by the fruit of good works. However, God does not redeem us and then send us on our way. Too many in the church, and likely at Galatia, believe that they have to produce their own good works. In contrast, Paul drives us to our union with Christ and the work of the Spirit. As Paul explains, "I have been crucified

Introduction

with Christ. It is no longer I who live, but Christ who lives in me" (Gal. 2:20). In other words, both justification and sanctification come by faith alone in Christ. We are no more sanctified by our good works than we are justified by them. Rather, we look by faith alone to Christ and he saves. As Paul makes clear, such an approach to redemption in no way mitigates the believer's need to produce good works. Instead, Paul desires to have the Galatians recognize that Christ is the source of their salvation—both in justification *and* sanctification.

Another topic Paul stresses in Galatians is eschatology, or *last things*. For many in the church, eschatology deals with the last days immediately before the return of Christ. However, Paul invokes Old Testament apocalyptic language from Isaiah 65–66 to demonstrate that the long-awaited new heavens and earth are not only a future but a *present* reality. They have dawned with the advent of Christ and his outpouring of the Holy Spirit. Hence, Paul stresses the fact that circumcision is a mark that belongs to the present evil age (Gal. 1:4) and the elementary principles of the world (Gal. 4:3, 9), and consequently it counts for nothing. Circumcision was part of the wall of division between Jew and Gentile that Christ has broken down.

The new creation does not begin at the conclusion of all things but in the middle of history. At the consummation, however, Christ will close the present evil age and the only thing that will be left is the new creation and those who are a part of it because of Christ's regenerating grace. In summary, Christ ushers in the new creation and only those in union with him will dwell in it. In the meantime, the Church is on a pilgrimage to the New Jerusalem as we follow Christ and walk by the Spirit, like Israel of old followed the pillar of cloud by day and fire by night.

Justification, sanctification, and eschatology do not exhaust all the truth contained in Galatians, but they do touch upon its main themes. Whereas the false teachers sought to bring division, strife, and a grace-enabled, but nevertheless man-centered, doctrine of salvation, Paul sets forth Christ as the one in whom there is neither Jew nor Greek, slave nor free, Jew nor Gentile, male nor female—the one in whom believers find deliverance from Satan, sin and death, and the present evil age. All other substitutes are false gospels! Hence, Paul's epistle to the Galatians beckons the reader to understand that anyone who advocates a gospel other than the gospel of Christ lies under the curse of God.

Before we proceed to the text, it is helpful to survey briefly the location and historical context of the Galatian churches, as well as Paul's relationship to them. Galatia was a large area in Asia Minor that now occupies modern-day Turkey. This location is mentioned in Acts 16:6, "And they went through the region of Phrygia and Galatia, having been forbidden by the Holy Spirit to speak the word in Asia," and 18:23, "After spending some time there, he departed and went from one place to the next through the region of Galatia and Phrygia, strengthening all the disciples." These verses reference the southern portion of the area which included Antioch of Pisidia and Iconium. Paul preached in these cities when he was on his first missionary journey (recounted in Acts 13–14).[2]

Paul and Barnabas were sent out by the church at Antioch (Acts 13:2–3). They sailed to Cyprus and preached "in the synagogues of the Jews" (Acts 13:4). They subsequently left Cyprus and traveled to Antioch of Pisidia where Paul once again preached at the synagogue (Acts 13:15). Although Paul preached among the Jews, the religious leaders "were filled with jealousy and began to contradict what was spoken by Paul, reviling him" (Acts 13:45). Paul announced that the gospel was not only for

---

2. Ralph P. Martin and Julie L. Wu, "Galatians," in *Zondervan Illustrated Bible Backgrounds Commentary,* 4 vols., ed. Clinton E. Arnold (Grand Rapids, MI: Zondervan, 2002), III:266–267.

the Jews but also for the Gentiles, and, upon hearing this, the Gentiles in the crowd "began rejoicing and glorifying the word of the Lord, and as many as were appointed to eternal life believed" (Acts 13:48). This turn of events infuriated many of the influential Jewish people of the city and they persecuted Paul and Barnabas, causing them to shake the dust from their feet and head off to Iconium in the region of Galatia (Acts 13:51).

Once in Galatia, Paul and Barnabas again proceeded to the Jewish synagogue "and spoke in such a way that a great number of both Jews and Greeks believed" (Acts 14:1). Despite opposition from unbelieving Jews, Paul and Barnabas remained among the Galatians "for a long time, speaking boldly for the Lord," but the unbelievers of the city soon prepared to kill them. Thus, they fled to other cities of Galatia, Lystra, Derbe, and Lycaonia and "there they continued to preach the gospel" (Acts 14:7). When they were in Lystra, Paul healed a man crippled from birth, which caused the people of the city to suppose that Paul and Barnabas were the gods Zeus and Hermes (Acts 14:8–18).

It was there in Lystra that the unbelieving crowds finally caught up with Paul, stoned him, dragged him outside the city, and left him for dead. Amazingly, the disciples found Paul alive, and he then proceeded with Barnabas on his missionary journey to another Galatian city, Derbe. There in Derbe, Paul "preached the gospel" and "made many disciples." Returning back through Lystra, Iconium, and Antioch, Paul endeavored to strengthen the Galatian churches that he and Barnabas had planted (Acts 14:19–23). They encouraged the churches in Galatia "to continue in the faith" even in the face of tribulation (Acts 14:22). Once Paul and Barnabas had appointed elders in every church, they committed the churches to the Lord, and then passed through Pisidia, Pamphylia, Perga, and Attalia, eventually returning to their departure point in Antioch. There in Antioch, they gave a report to the church and "declared all that God had done with them, and how he had opened a door of faith to the Gentiles" (Acts 14:27). Given Paul's heavy involvement in the planting of the Galatian churches, it is unsurprising that he was so concerned to warn them of false teaching.

Galatians

I

No Other Gospel

GALATIANS 1:1–9

Paul, an apostle—not from men nor through man, but through Jesus Christ and God the Father, who raised him from the dead— and all the brothers who are with me, To the churches of Galatia: Grace to you and peace from God our Father and the Lord Jesus Christ, who gave himself for our sins to deliver us from the present evil age, according to the will of our God and Father, to whom be the glory forever and ever. Amen.

Paul's epistle to the Galatian churches is famous as much for the apostle's fiery tone as for its doctrinal content. Paul is greatly agitated in this epistle, and for good reason. The churches that he planted in and around Galatia were departing from the gospel. They were on the dangerous path of apostasy. Paul's agitation, therefore, should not be likened to an oppressive or angry master who verbally abuses his subordinates. Rather, Paul is like a distressed parent who cries out to stop a meandering child from heading into a busy street, knowing that the child's life is in great peril. In the case of the Galatians, however, the dan-

1

gers are far greater than physical harm or even death; the stakes are high—apostasy and its consequent, eternal damnation. Just because Paul took on a fiery tone, we should not assume that he hated the Galatians. Rather, as the sixteenth-century Reformed theologian Wolfgang Musculus once observed:

> When calling the erring churches of the faithful back to the right way, the apostle is not lacking the abundance of God's grace any more than he lacked it when, by his preaching, he was calling unbelievers, ungodly people and strangers to Christ to share in heavenly grace and eternal life.[1]

In other words, love and rebuke are in no way antithetical.

But how did this situation in Galatia arise? How did the Galatian churches begin to toy with apostasy? Perhaps some brief background information would be helpful.

First, we know from Acts 13–14 that Paul planted the Galatian churches during what was likely his first missionary journey.[2] Second, shortly after Paul had departed, false teachers descended upon the churches, personally attacked Paul (Gal. 4:17), and preached a false gospel (Gal. 1:6–7). These false teachers taught that circumcision was necessary for salvation (Gal. 6:12). Since the Galatian churches were largely composed of Gentiles (non-Jews), the false teachers taught that converts not only had to believe in Christ for their salvation but also had to be circumcised (Gal. 2:3–5; 5:2, 6, 11; 6:12–15).

Circumcision was the sign of the covenant in the Old Testament before the advent of Christ (Gen. 17), and reversion to this sign was indicative of serious confusion about the nature of salvation. So, then, Paul was writing to the Galatian church-

---

1. Gerald L. Bray, ed., *Galatians, Ephesians*, vol. 10, *Reformation Commentary on Scripture, New Testament* (Downers Grove, IL: IVP Academic, 2011), 18.

2. See Thomas R. Schreiner, *Galatians*, ZECNT (Grand Rapids, MI: Zondervan, 2010), 22–31.

es to correct these grave problems. In this letter, but especially in the passage before us, Paul sets forth the importance and exclusivity of the gospel of Christ, a message that has abiding relevance even in our own day.

The Initial Greeting

The beginning of Paul's epistle bears similarities to all of the other letters that we find in the New Testament. At the outset, Paul identifies himself as an apostle, one commissioned by Jesus Christ to preach and propagate the gospel. The gospel is the message of Christ's life, death, resurrection, and ascension, which is the power of salvation for those who believe in him, first for the Jew and then for the Gentile (cf. Rom. 1:16–17).[3] Paul emphasizes the saving nature of the gospel of Christ in verses 3–4: "Grace to you and peace from God our Father and the Lord Jesus Christ, who gave himself for our sins to deliver us from the present evil age."

The gospel is a manifestation of God's grace, his favor that is poured out upon sinners without the slightest reference to their merit. Not only is the gospel a manifestation of God's grace, but it is also that which brings peace to God's people (cf. Num. 6:24–26). Before a person is saved, God is his enemy; the sinner is under God's judgment and wrath, and there is no peace between him and his Maker. Yet, when God sets his grace upon a person and enables him to believe, the sinner is no longer at enmity with God—Christ, the only Savior, has brought peace. God the Father gave us his Son, and the Son gave himself for our sins, "to deliver us from the present evil age" (Gal. 1:4b). What does Paul mean by "the present evil age"?

---

3. On the importance of the inclusion of the ascension of Christ as a distinct event from his resurrection, see Douglas Farrow, *Ascension and Ecclesia: On the Significance of the Doctrine of the Ascension for Ecclesiology and Christian Cosmology* (Edinburgh: T&T Clark, 1999), 1–40.

The present evil age is the fallen reign of the first Adam, which is now subject to Satan, sin, and death. In a word, the present evil age is the kingdom of darkness. Notice, then, that through believing in Christ we are delivered out from under the dominion of Satan, sin, and death, and are transferred into the kingdom of light, or, as it is also known, the *age to come* (cf. Matt. 12:32; Mark 10:30; Luke 18:30; Col. 1:13; Heb. 6:5).[4] At this point we might not immediately detect that Paul is upset, since this epistle opens in much the same way as his other letters, but his agitation is evidenced by two peculiar elements.

First, at the very outset, Paul points out that his apostleship is "not from men nor through man, but through Jesus Christ." The fact that Paul is compelled to remind the Galatians of the source of his apostolic authority is an important hint. His message is not of human but of divine—and more specifically, christological—origin: Paul was commissioned and ordained by Christ himself on the road to Damascus (Acts 9:1–25).[5]

Second, after Paul praises God on the heels of announcing the redemption given through Christ, he does not segue to thanksgiving and prayer as he does in nearly every other letter, but to rebuke. In his other epistles, Paul gives thanks for the church to whom he writes and even makes mention that he prays for them (1 Cor. 1:4; Eph. 1:15ff; Phil. 1:3ff; Col. 1:3ff; 1 Thess. 1:2ff; 2 Thess. 1:3ff; 2 Tim. 1:3ff; Philem. 4ff). But it seems that there are more pressing matters on Paul's mind.

The Exclusivity of the Gospel

Paul's overriding concern is the Galatian apostasy. Paul writes: "I am astonished that you are so quickly deserting him who called you in the grace of Christ and are turning to a differ-

4. See Geerhardus Vos, *The Pauline Eschatology* (Phillipsburg, NJ: P&R, [1930] 1979), 1–41.

5. On the theological significance of Paul's conversion, see Seyoon Kim, *The Origin of Paul's Gospel* (Grand Rapids, MI: Eerdmans, 1982).

ent gospel—not that there is another one, but there are some who trouble you and want to distort the gospel of Christ" (Gal. 1:6–7). While we do not know just how quickly the Galatians abandoned the gospel, it happened quickly enough to astonish Paul. And, make no mistake about it, the Galatians had turned to "a different gospel."

Paul immediately qualifies what he means by *a different gospel*; it is certainly not that there are other *legitimate* gospels. Rather, the Galatians have departed from the one true gospel and embraced a distorted and false message. From the outset, both Paul's great concern and the great danger threatening the Galatians is evident. Part of the reason behind Paul's alarm is, no doubt, that this threat to the gospel has come from *within* the church—demons dressed as angels, if you will. Martin Luther describes the danger of such a threat:

> Here let us learn to recognize the tricks and craft of the devil. A heretic does not come with the label of "error" or "devil"; nor does the devil himself come in the form of a devil, especially not that "white devil." In fact, even the black devil, who impels men to overt acts of evil, provide them with a covering for the acts they perpetrate or intend to perpetrate. In his fury the murderer does not see that murder is as great and horrible a sin as it is in fact, because he has a covering for it. Lechers, thieves, covetous men, drunkards, and the like, have the means to flatter themselves and cover up their sins. Thus the black devil always emerges in the disguise and covering of all his works and tricks. But in the spiritual area, where Satan emerges not black but white, in the guise of an angel or even of God himself, there he puts himself forward with very sly pretense and amazing tricks. He peddles his deadly poison as the doctrine of grace, the Word of God, and the Gospel of Christ. This is why Paul calls

> the doctrine of the false apostles and ministers of Satan a "gospel," saying, "to a different gospel."[6]

Regardless of good intentions or a purported devotion to God's Word, people can distort and corrupt the gospel, and even worse, lead *others* into falsehood.

Paul insists that the gospel of Jesus Christ is unchanging; he makes this emphatic point twice: "But even if we or an angel from heaven should preach to you a gospel contrary to the one we preached to you, let him be accursed. As we have said before, so now I say again: If anyone is preaching to you a gospel contrary to the one you received, let him be accursed" (Gal. 1:8–9). Think about what Paul has said for a moment. He rules out the possibility that any human being can come along and change the message of the gospel, even one of the apostles. Paul also rules out the possibility that a heavenly being can come along and change the message of the gospel. Additionally, the person or angelic being that preaches a different gospel lies under God's curse (*anathema*)—he is the object of God's judgment and wrath (cf. 1 Cor. 16:22; Rom. 9:3; Lev. 27:28–29; Num. 18:14; Deut. 7:26; Exod. 22:20; Num. 21:2–3).[7]

There are several things we should notice about the way Paul has opened his letter to the Galatian churches, as they relate to the nature and exclusivity of the gospel of Christ. Notice the nature of the gospel. The gospel of Jesus Christ is the announcement of the good news. And what exactly is that good news? It begins with some *bad* news: man is sinful, and his sin not only separates him from God but also renders him liable to God's wrath and judgment. Sin, whether great or small, separates us from God and makes us liable to his just judgment.

---

6. Martin Luther, *Galatians*, vol. 26, *Luther's Works*, ed. Jaroslav Pelikan (St. Louis: Concordia, 1963), 49.

7. Schreiner, *Galatians*, 87.

No Other Gospel

The *good* news is that God has sent his Son to deliver us from this present evil age. Jesus Christ has come and lived his life in perfect obedience to the demands of the law, which means he has fulfilled the requirements of the law on behalf of those who look to him by faith. Jesus has suffered and died on the cross to pay the penalty and debt that sinful people owe, on behalf of those who trust him by faith. Jesus was raised from the dead to signal his sinlessness and righteousness, to show that God had accepted his sacrifice on behalf of the people of God, and to prophetically declare that all who look to him by faith will be likewise raised. This is the gospel of Jesus Christ. It is our salvation—accomplished and applied.

Paul writes that it was God's will, not man's will, to pour out his grace and mercy upon undeserving sinners like us by sending his Son so that we might be delivered from this present evil age. We are transferred from the kingdom of darkness into the kingdom of light, and this occurs by God's grace alone through faith alone in Christ alone. The gospel is the difference between heaven and hell. Yet it seems that in every age, the enemy has tried to cloud and obscure the message of the gospel of Christ. Certainly this was true in Paul's day.

What made the situation more alarming was that the false gospel was not coming from the easily identifiable enemies of Christ from *outside* the church, but from *within*, from those who professed to follow him. If we think that the church has progressed beyond such pitfalls, we should think again. Katharine Jefferts Schori, the presiding bishop of the Episcopal Church of the USA, was asked in an interview, "Is belief in Jesus the only way to get to heaven?" She responded, "We who practice the Christian tradition understand him as our vehicle to the divine. But for us to assume that God could not act in other ways, is, I think, to put God in an awfully small box."[8] Her statement indi-

---

8. Jeff Chu, "10 Questions for Katharine Jefferts Schori," *Time*, July 17, 2006, 6.

cates that she has either misunderstood Paul, which is unlikely given Paul's absolute clarity, or she simply does not believe him.

We must never forget the source of Paul's authority—an apostle, not from men nor through man, but through Jesus Christ and God the Father (v. 1). Paul was an ambassador directly appointed by God the Son, the very image of God the Father, to preach the gospel, the good news. Moreover, Paul has said that anyone who preaches a gospel different than the one he and the apostles had delivered stands under God's curse. We do not put God in a "small box" when we stand upon the gospel as God has delivered it through Christ by the Spirit to his ambassadors, the apostles. Rather, sinful people try to confine God in a small box of their own making by saying that Christ is not the only way to salvation: Is Christ's salvation so small that other ways to God are necessary?

Such beliefs about Christ are heretical. J. Gresham Machen (1881–1937), the founder of Westminster Theological Seminary and the Orthodox Presbyterian Church, exposed the folly of such liberalism:

> It may appear that what the liberal theologian has retained after abandoning to the enemy one Christian doctrine after another is not Christianity at all, but a religion which is so entirely different from Christianity as to belong in a distinct category. It may appear further that the fears of the modern man as to Christianity were entirely ungrounded, and that in abandoning the embattled walls of the city of God he has fled in needless panic into the open plains of a vague natural religion only to fall an easy victim to the enemy who ever lies in ambush there.[9]

---

9. J. Gresham Machen, *Christianity and Liberalism* (Grand Rapids, MI: Eerdmans, [1923] 1999), 6–7.

No Other Gospel

If we have any doubts about Machen's evaluation, all we need to do is read Ms. Schori's answer to the question of what her focus is for the Episcopal Church. Ms. Schori responds: "Our focus needs to be on feeding people who are hungry, on providing primary education to girls and boys, on healing people with AIDS, on addressing tuberculosis and malaria, on sustainable development. That ought to be the primary focus."[10] What is missing? The gospel of Jesus Christ! Here, the head of the Episcopalian Church, 2.3 million members strong, does not even mention the gospel. A whole "church," at least to the extent that its bishop accurately represents it, has completely forsaken the gospel. Indeed, it has turned to another gospel—salvation through humanitarianism, which is basically salvation by good works. But the corruption of the gospel is not confined to "the liberals." We should realize that we too can fall into similar sins.

Meditate upon Paul's opening words and recognize the nature of the gospel. It is the salvation of God through Christ applied by the Holy Spirit to deliver us *from* this present evil age and *into* the age to come, the kingdom of God. Regardless of the origins of error, whether from within the Church or without, we must be vigilant to protect the purity of the gospel. We must herald the *exclusivity* of the gospel, the saving work of Jesus Christ on behalf of sinners. We must be willing, in humility and with love, to confront the sinners of this world so that they will see their sin and turn to Christ. In the end, with Paul, our desire should be to lift high the gospel of Jesus Christ to the glory of our triune Lord, to whom be the glory forever and ever.

---

10. Chu, "Ten Questions," 6.

2

Called by God

GALATIANS 1:10–24

For am I now seeking the approval of man, or of God? Or am I trying to please man? If I were still trying to please man, I would not be a servant of Christ. For I would have you know, brothers, that the gospel that was preached by me is not man's gospel. For I did not receive it from any man, nor was I taught it, but I received it through a revelation of Jesus Christ.

In the first century, there were many people who persecuted Christians for their faith in Christ. One such person was Saul of Tarsus, or as we now know him, the apostle Paul. The challenge for Paul was that people knew that he initially wanted to destroy the church but they were now hearing reports that he was preaching the very faith he once tried to destroy. As one can imagine, people were likely suspicious of Paul. Were his actions genuine? Were his motives pure? At the same time, some people probably wondered about the origins of his authority. Did anyone authorize Paul to preach the gospel? What did the other apostles think? The false teachers in Galatia likely tried

11

to exploit this apparent weakness in Paul's ministry. This is why Paul addresses the origins of his apostolic authority: a personal commission by Jesus Christ—a commission that extended from Israel to the ends of the earth. These two things, Paul's commission and the international scope of the gospel, have important implications for both the gospel and the mission of the Church.

Divine Origins of Paul's Gospel and Authority

Paul begins by explaining that his only interest is pleasing Christ: "For am I now seeking the approval of man, or of God? Or am I trying to please man? If I were still trying to please man, I would not be a servant of Christ" (Gal. 1:10). Paul desired to be a faithful herald of the message he had been commissioned to deliver. Moreover, Paul states for a second time that the gospel was not of human origin: "For I would have you know, brothers, that the gospel that was preached by me is not man's gospel. For I did not receive it from any man, nor was I taught it, but I received it through a revelation of Jesus Christ" (Gal. 1:11–12). Let us take note that this is one of the first characteristics of the gospel.

Paul was not commissioned by the Church, nor was he commissioned by man, nor did he assume his commission by self-appointment. Instead, Paul was confronted on the road to Damascus by the risen Christ, who personally commissioned Paul to preach the gospel (Acts 9:1–25). This is why Paul says that he received the gospel "through a revelation of Jesus Christ." Paul sets the backdrop for his call by reminding the Galatians of his former life, as one who was a Pharisee of Pharisees and even a persecutor of the Church. Among his peers, Paul was matchless—he was circumcised on the eighth day in accordance with the law, of the tribe of Benjamin, and according to his own testimony, a "Hebrew of Hebrews" (Phil. 3:5–6). In fact, Paul testifies that he was "educated at the feet of Gamaliel," one of the foremost rabbis of his day, and raised

Called by God

"according to the strict manner of the law of our fathers" (Acts 22:3). In other words, Paul was deeply concerned to preserve and protect the faith of Israel. However, Paul's zeal was not ultimately for the Word of God and the Messiah but, in a telling statement, he admits that his passion was for the "traditions of my fathers" (v. 14). At this point, we are beginning to see hints of the brewing Galatian heresy—it has something to do with the traditions of the Jews rather than the gospel of Jesus Christ. In other words, Paul had broken with Judaism, while his opponents still promoted these traditions.

God set his sights on Paul and commissioned him to preach the gospel through his Son:

> But when he who had set me apart before I was born, and who called me by his grace, was pleased to reveal his Son to me, in order that I might preach him among the Gentiles, I did not immediately consult with anyone; nor did I go up to Jerusalem to those who were apostles before me, but I went away into Arabia, and returned again to Damascus. (Galatians 1:15–17)

Paul places great emphasis upon the divine origins of his commission in language that echoes the calls of Old Testament prophets: "Before I formed you in the womb I knew you, and before you were born I consecrated you; I appointed you a prophet to the nations" (Jer. 1:5). It appears that Paul has Jeremiah's call in mind, especially given the similarity of the two calls—both Jeremiah and Paul were appointed as *prophets to the nations*. Before we proceed, however, there are several other things about Paul's statement in verses 15–17 to consider.

Paul did not consult with anyone concerning his commission; he did not go up to Jerusalem to confer with the apostles. Instead he went to Arabia and later Damascus. Scholars have speculated for centuries as to what Paul did in Arabia and Damascus for those three years. Some think he went away to contemplate the revelation of Christ that he had seen, others that he was personally instructed by Christ in the wilderness. Martin Luther offers his thoughts on the matter in his usual brusque but insightful manner: "It is silly . . . to ask what Paul did in Arabia. What else would he have done but preach Christ?"[1] We will never really know what happened, but we should not let our curiosity concerning these three years obscure the point. Paul is emphatic—his commission was directly from Christ, not in any way from man, not even the other apostles.

The Scope of the Gospel

Keeping the christological origins of the gospel and Paul's commission in mind, we can consider the scope of the gospel. Remember, Paul was set apart from birth to preach to the Gentiles, to anyone who was not a Jew, which echoes Jeremiah's call to be a prophet to the nations. In fact, the Greek word translated "gentiles" (*ethne*) could accurately be rendered "nations." This is important information, as it immediately establishes the far-reaching purpose of the gospel. The gospel is not parochial, limited to one region, or something restricted to Israel and the Jewish people, or to interested parties. Rather, the gospel has an international outlook.

Paul was set apart from the womb by the sovereign choice of God so that he might preach the gospel to the nations. Recall that the nations have been the object of the gospel from the very outset of redemptive history. This international scope arises in the covenant promise to Abraham—the blessings of God's covenant with him would extend to many nations: "And I will make of you a great nation, and I will bless you and make your name great, so that you will be a blessing. I will bless those who bless you, and him who dishonors you I will curse, and in

---

1. Gerald L. Bray, ed., *Galatians, Ephesians*, vol. 10, *Reformation Commentary on Scripture, New Testament* (Downers Grove, IL: IVP Academic, 2011), 41.

you all the families of the earth shall be blessed" (Gen. 12:2–3). In another parallel to the Old Testament prophets, Paul's prenatal allocation to God's sovereign purposes resembles the call of Isaiah, which itself was ultimately prophetic of Christ: "The LORD called me from the womb, from the body of my mother he named my name" (Isa 49:1). The prophet also writes: "He says: 'It is too light a thing that you should be my servant to raise up the tribes of Jacob and to bring back the preserved of Israel; I will make you as a light for the nations, that my salvation may reach to the end of the earth'" (Isa. 49:6). There is also the Great Commission, in which Christ commands the Church to take the gospel into the nations (Matt. 28:18–20). Clearly, the gospel was intended to go forth to the nations, and Paul was God's chosen instrument to carry out this task. At the same time, the scope of the gospel also says something about the nature of Christ's reign. The nations are supposed to submit to Christ (cf. Ps. 2). All of these elements continue to hint at the nature of the problem at Galatia.

The false teachers, the Judaizers, insisted that Christian Gentile converts had to believe in Christ *and* receive the sign of circumcision in order to be saved. More or less, though there are certainly other important details that we will explore in the following chapters, the Judaizers taught that Gentiles had to become Jewish to be saved. But if the scope of the gospel is international, then we must seriously doubt the notion that the nations would have to convert to Judaism. This idea is contrary to the Scriptures for two main reasons.

First, to receive circumcision in addition to faith in Christ was a rejection of the perfect sufficiency of Christ's work as the ground for a person's salvation. Saying a person had to be circumcised was an attempt to add the believer's law-keeping to the perfect law-keeping of Christ. Second, to insist that circumcision was a prerequisite for salvation was an attempt to turn back the clock of redemptive history and revert to life under the Mosaic covenant. It was to return to the bondage of the law and its requirements—bondage from which the people of God had been freed by Christ.

Second, it was taking a step back into "the present evil age," back into the darkness. If Paul's ministry was the outworking of God's purposes foretold in Isaiah 49, then the propagation of the gospel as a light unto the nations was the arrival of the kingdom of God—the long awaited eschatological kingdom. Or more simply, it was the arrival of the gospel of Christ—heaven come down among the nations of the earth. Why would the Galatians want to retreat and return to the bondage of the law?

The Essence of the Gospel

Is the gospel made effective through our obedience to the law, or by the obedience of Christ? The right answer is the latter: Christ's obedience secures our salvation. That our salvation hinges upon faith alone in Christ alone is evident even in Paul's autobiographical defense of his ministry, which is, in effect, a defense of the gospel. Paul tells the Galatians that he later visited Jerusalem with the intention of meeting the apostles, but that he met with only Peter and James, the half-brother of Christ. Again, Paul emphasizes the origin of his authority—it is not from the apostles but from Christ alone. He then says he went into the regions of Syria and Cilicia and preached to the churches in Judea.

These churches, as we can well imagine, marveled that Paul was now preaching the very gospel that he had once despised. Notice specifically what Paul preached: "the faith he once tried to destroy'" (Gal. 1:23). The people to whom Paul preached said that he was preaching the *faith*. In other words, salvation comes not through our obedience but by faith alone in Jesus Christ. Our salvation is not introspective, where we look within to our own abilities and our own obedience. Rather, our salvation is *extraspective*, in that we look without to the abilities and obedience of Christ.[2]

Paul closes the chapter by writing: "And they glorified God because of me" (Gal. 1:24). What was the goal of the propagation of the gospel according to the prophet Isaiah? The prophet states: "And he said to me, 'You are my servant, Israel, in whom I will be glorified'" (Isa 49:3). Isaiah's words were ultimately spoken of Christ, God's perfect servant, in whom the nations would rise up and glorify the one and only true God, and it was Christ, working in and through Paul by the preaching of the gospel, that caused the nations, the Gentiles, to rejoice in the salvation extended to them.

Christ for the Nations

As we reflect upon the things Paul has written in defense of his ministry and the gospel, I hope we are struck by a sense of the grandeur and magnitude of the gospel, as well as our own responsibility in propagating it throughout the world. We should recognize that the gospel is not of human but divine origins. Regardless of man's attempts to marginalize the gospel by saying that it is a myth or that it is merely "one way" among others, we must stand firm upon the truth that it is the *only* way we can be saved. Jesus Christ, the uncreated image of God, God in the flesh, personally commissioned the apostles, and especially Paul, to carry the gospel into the nations. The gospel was no late invention or plan B; rather, from the very beginning of redemptive history, it has been God's stated intention and plan to bring salvation to the nations.

Though we may not have been commissioned by Christ in the same manner that Paul was, we as a corporate body *have*

---

2. John Murray coined the term *extraspective*. See John Murray, *The Epistle to the Romans*, NICNT (Grand Rapids, MI: Eerdmans, 1968), 123.

been commissioned. That corporate commission, of course, is
one that should be familiar to us all:

> And Jesus came and said to them, "All authority in
> heaven and on earth has been given to me. Go there-
> fore and make disciples of all nations, baptizing
> them in the name of the Father and of the Son and
> of the Holy Spirit, teaching them to observe all that
> I have commanded you. And behold, I am with you
> always, to the end of the age." (Matthew 28:18–20)

As a corporate body, our prayers, tithes, offerings, and support
should be given to the Church to see that it carries out this
commission. The church cannot carry out the commission un-
less she sends out ministers of the Word to preach the gospel
to the nations.

As individuals, we should pray to be given opportunities
to share the gospel with others through personal evangelism.
All too often, we know intellectually that the nations should
receive the gospel, but our prayers mention little to nothing
about the gospel spreading throughout the world. True, God
has ordained that the elect will believe in Christ. However,
God ordains both the ends and the means by which his decree
of election is brought to pass. In this respect, prayer is one of
the chief pillars of the conversion of the lost. We should pray
along with Isaac Watts's hymn, "How Sweet and Awesome is
the Place":

> Pity the nations, O our God,
> Constrain the earth to come;
> Send thy victorious Word abroad,
> And bring the strangers home.
>
> We long to see thy churches full,
> That all the chosen race
> may, with one voice and heart and soul,
> sing thy redeeming grace.

In the end, however, the evangelization of the world is not itself the final goal of the Church's commission. Remember, Paul bases his call and mission on the direct commission of Christ, which had its roots in the Isaianic prophecies: "You are my servant, Israel, in whom I will be glorified" (Isa. 49:3). Ultimately, the purpose of the gospel is worship—the worship and praise of our triune Lord. John Piper captures this point well when he writes:

> Missions is not the ultimate goal of the church. Worship is. Missions exists because worship doesn't. Worship is ultimate, not missions, because God is ultimate, not man. When this age is over, and the countless millions of the redeemed fall on their faces before the throne of God, missions will be no more. It is a temporary necessity. But worship abides forever.[3]

Worship was the response of the churches in Judea when they learned that Paul was preaching the gospel—they glorified God. Our desire, therefore, should not be that the gospel would make people's lives better, but ultimately that the nations would come to God's temple and worship him. Again, prophecies from long ago foretold of a time when in the "latter days" the "mountain of the house of the Lord" would be established and the nations (*ethne* LXX) would flow to it to worship Yahweh (Isa. 2:2–3). Paul's ministry was prima facie evidence that these prophetic words were now being fulfilled.

As we continue to study Paul's letter, ask the Lord that he would grant you a greater understanding of the gospel. Do not forget its divine origin. Do not forget that it is the power unto salvation first for the Jew and then the Gentile. Pray that the gospel would go into all the nations.

---

3. See John Piper, *Let the Nations Be Glad: The Supremacy of God in Missions* (Grand Rapids, MI: Baker, 1993), 11.

3

Paul Accepted by the Apostles

GALATIANS 2:1–10

But even Titus, who was with me, was not forced to be circumcised, though he was a Greek. Yet because of false brothers secretly brought in—who slipped in to spy out our freedom that we have in Christ Jesus, so that they might bring us into slavery— to them we did not yield in submission even for a moment, so that the truth of the gospel might be preserved for you.

A seal of approval can instill confidence in a consumer's heart. If a customer has doubts about whether a product is worth the price, a celebrity endorsement might make the difference. For this reason, companies seeking a consumer's hard-earned money will hire the best, brightest, and most popular stars to endorse their products. Something similar to this was going on in the Galatian churches. False teachers had sown a number of doubts concerning the authenticity of Paul's ministry—the validity of his endorsement. Paul, therefore, set out to defend his ministry and show that the apostles accepted him as one of their own. At the same time, however, Paul also wanted to emphasize that his commission was not from any man—the other apostles simply *acknowledged* that Christ had personally commissioned him.

Paul began in the previous passage with a defense of his commission as an apostle—he emphasized that he received his commission neither from men, through men, from the church, nor from the apostles. Nor was he self-appointed: he was personally commissioned by the resurrected and ascended Christ. Paul also explained that he was appointed from his mother's womb to be a prophet to the nations. In other words, from the outset, Paul lays the foundation that the gospel has always been intended for the nations and that it was never meant to be restricted to Israel. When Paul, one who formerly persecuted the church, preached the very faith that he intended to destroy, the churches to whom he preached glorified God.

In the passage before us, Paul continues to defend his ministry, although we must keep in mind that it is not so much a defense of himself as it is a defense of his Christ-given call. This means Paul is simultaneously defending the gospel of Jesus Christ and his authority in the Church. Paul's defense of his ministry centers on three things. First, he brings Titus forward as a living example of the nature of the gospel. Second, he explains that the apostles, especially James, Peter, and John, accepted him as an apostle. Third, the original apostles and Paul were together constructing the church, the final dwelling place of God, with both Jews and Gentiles.

Titus: A Living Example

Paul continues his defense of his ministry with an autobiographical account of what happened in the years following his commission by Christ. We know that he did not immediately go

Paul Accepted by the Apostles

up to Jerusalem but instead went into Arabia and Damascus for three years. Afterwards, he went to Jerusalem and met James, the half-brother of Christ, and Peter, and then proceeded to preach in the churches of Judea. Fourteen years went by before he returned again to Jerusalem. Notice that this is yet more evidence that Paul's commission did not depend upon the apostles but upon Christ, as he was conducting his ministry for some fourteen years apart from the supervision or approval of the apostles. Paul nevertheless went up to Jerusalem and brought both Barnabas and Titus with him.

Titus's presence with Paul was significant because Titus was "a Greek" (v. 3). Titus was a Gentile, and he looked to Christ by faith alone for his salvation. However, note what Paul says about Titus and his uncircumcised state: "But even Titus, who was with me, was not forced to be circumcised, though he was a Greek" (Gal. 2:3). Paul specifically communicates that Titus was not forced to be circumcised. We find out from Paul, then, the nature of the Galatian heresy. Jews who professed to follow Jesus were insisting, if not even forcing, Gentile Christians to be circumcised. In other words, they could not be saved apart from faith *and* circumcision. Yet, here is Paul, Pharisee of Pharisees, educated in the Old Testament, zealous for the traditions of his fathers, but accompanied by an *uncircumcised* Gentile convert. How could Paul, a circumcised Jew and former Pharisee, allow a Gentile to become party to the covenant of Abraham without receiving the the sign of the covenant—circumcision?

The answer comes in Paul's critique of the false teachers: "Yet because of false brothers secretly brought in—who slipped in to spy out our freedom that we have in Christ Jesus, so that they might bring us into slavery—to them we did not yield in submission even for a moment, so that the truth of the gospel might be preserved for you" (Gal. 2:4–5). Paul contended that circumcision was no longer necessary because Christ had come—Christ fulfilled the law and the prophets. He came not only to render his obedience to the law but also came to fulfill the shadows of the ceremonial law, which all pointed to Christ.

Circumcision ultimately pointed to the redemption that would come through Christ: "In him also you were circumcised with a circumcision made without hands, by putting off the body of the flesh, by the circumcision of Christ" (Col. 2:11; cf. Luke 12:50; Gen. 17:14; Isa. 53:8; Jer. 11:19). This is why Paul had no problem with Titus's uncircumcised state. Moreover, this is why Paul says that he did not yield in submission to the false teachers on this matter even for a moment—so that the truth of the gospel would be preserved. Paul knew that if he had Titus circumcised, he would be returning Titus and himself to the bondage and slavery of the law and its requirement for perfect obedience.

The Acceptance of the Apostles

When Paul finally met with the apostles, Peter, James, and John, Christ's original inner circle (cf. Mark 5:37; 9:2; 14:33; Luke 9:28), they saw and recognized his commission: "When they saw that I had been entrusted with the gospel to the uncircumcised, just as Peter had been entrusted with the gospel to the circumcised (for he who worked through Peter for his apostolic ministry to the circumcised worked also through me for mine to the Gentiles)" (Gal. 2:7–8).

It is important to notice that the apostles did not commission or ordain Paul to his ministry. Jesus personally commissioned and ordained him. Even though they did not ordain Paul to his ministry, they recognized that he had been personally called by Jesus just as they themselves had been called. The only difference was that Christ called Peter to labor among the Jews, and Paul the Gentiles. Nevertheless, the same Christ was sending forth the gospel through both Peter and Paul to both Jew and Gentile alike. To emphasize this point, the apostles gave Paul the right hand of fellowship: "And when James and Cephas and John, who seemed to be pillars, perceived the grace that was given to me, they gave the right hand of fellowship to Barnabas and me, that we should go to the Gentiles and they to the circumcised" (Gal. 2:9). Paul originally went to Jerusalem, not to receive apostolic sanction but to ensure they understood his divine appointment: "And from those who seemed to be influential (what they were makes no difference to me; God shows no partiality)—those, I say, who seemed influential added nothing to me" (Gal. 2:6). This was not in any way arrogance on Paul's part, but *confidence*—a confidence in the appointment and authority of Christ.

The Church Composed of Jews and Gentiles

Last but not least, the apostles were called to construct the church, the final dwelling place of God. Paul makes this point discretely, however, and some might not immediately recognize the language that he uses. I think people often read verse 9 with contemporary spectacles: "And when James and Cephas and John, who seemed to be pillars, perceived the grace that was given to me, they gave the right hand of fellowship to Barnabas and me, that we should go to the Gentiles and they to the circumcised" (Gal. 2:9). We read that James, Peter, and John were "pillars" (*stulos*) and we hear a word that we might use in our own context, namely that a prominent and upstanding person is called a "pillar" of society. This begins to approach what Paul has in mind, but there is far more signified by *pillar* here.

First, any Jew familiar with the Greek Old Testament, the Septuagint, would likely recognize the word, as it is the same word used for the pillars in Solomon's temple (1 Kings 7:15–22, LXX). In fact, the pillars were famous, even having proper names: "He set up the pillars at the vestibule of the temple. He set up the pillar on the south and called its name Jachin, and he set up the pillar on the north and called its name Boaz" (1 Kings 7:21). So, Paul uses an architectural term from Israel's past laden with significance.

Second, Ezekiel and Haggai prophesy of a time when God would rebuild his temple: "The latter glory of this house shall be greater than the former, says the LORD of hosts. And in this place I will give peace, declares the LORD of hosts" (Hag. 2:9; cf. Ezek. 47). Third, there is the testimony of Christ: "Jesus answered them, 'Destroy this temple, and in three days I will raise it up.' The Jews then said, 'It has taken forty-six years to build this temple, and will you raise it up in three days?' But he was speaking about the temple of his body" (John 2:19–21).

When we combine all of these texts, it is no surprise that both Peter and Paul use this same temple typology and apply it to the construction of the Church, the final temple: "You yourselves like living stones are being built up as a spiritual house, to be a holy priesthood, to offer spiritual sacrifices acceptable to God through Jesus Christ" (1 Pet. 2:5). In Paul's letter to the Ephesians, he writes:

> So then you are no longer strangers and aliens, but you are fellow citizens with the saints and members of the household of God, built on the foundation of the apostles and prophets, Christ Jesus himself being the cornerstone, in whom the whole structure, being joined together, grows into a holy temple in the Lord. In him you also are being built together into a dwelling place for God by the Spirit. (Ephesians 2:19–22)

What Paul says in Ephesians underlies his actions and interaction with the apostles. Paul came to the pillars of the final temple, God's dwelling place—to Peter, James, and John—and received the right hand of fellowship. Both Paul and the other apostles were building God's final dwelling place together, and it would consist of living stones, both Jews and Gentiles who looked to Christ alone by faith alone to receive redemption and be incorporated into the temple.

As we stop to ponder the significance of what Paul has written here, we should recognize how his arguments refute the false teachers. The example of Titus, Paul's reception among the apostles, and his status as co-builder of the Church, with the apostles, out of both Jews and Gentiles, all worked together to refute the idea that Paul's apostolic ministry was inferior or that he was somehow preaching a different gospel than the rest of the apostles. Both Paul and the apostles, whether to the Jews or to the Gentiles, were preaching the very same gospel: that one is saved by grace alone through faith alone in Christ alone. This helps us to see the immediate significance of Paul's argument. More broadly, I hope we can appreciate the shocking nature of what Paul writes: *Gentiles* have now been incorporated into the people of God.

Place yourselves in the shoes of a first-century Jew for a moment. You have read the Old Testament and heard the command that a man must be circumcised to be a part of the covenant of Abraham, and if he is not, then he is cursed and must be cut off from the covenant (Gen. 17:10–14). You know that the pagan occupying forces of Antiochus Epiphanes (ca. 215– 164 B.C.) persecuted your ancestors and even killed them because of the sign of the covenant (1 Macc. 1:48; 1:60; 2 Macc. 6:1–11). There were even Jews who, in an attempt to escape the Gentile persecution, reversed circumcision through a surgical procedure (1 Macc. 1:11–15). And now Paul (along with the other apostles) begins preaching that circumcision is no longer a requirement for membership in the covenant of Abraham. You'd probably have something like this to say about Paul: "This man never ceases to speak words against this holy place and the law, for we have heard him say that this Jesus of Nazareth will destroy this place and will change the customs that Moses delivered to us" (Acts 6:13–14). Paul's message, therefore, was shocking to many. Jews were prepared to embrace Christ, but not prepared to forsake the sign of the covenant and the old traditions. What they did not realize is that circumcision did not and could not save them.

Rather, circumcision pointed forward to the saving work of Christ, who himself underwent the curse of the covenant. The cutting away of the foreskin symbolized either cutting away the body of sin or being cut off from the covenant community. Christ bore the curse on our behalf—and his death becomes our death and his life gives us life. This is what the false teachers and many of the Jews in Paul's day failed to grasp—the earth-shattering significance of Christ's work. Christ did this not only for the Jews but also for the Gentiles, for anyone who looks to him by faith. This is something that so many churchgoers still fail to grasp, namely, that salvation is and always has been by faith alone in Christ alone.

But we should also consider that Paul and the disciples were building the final temple, the church of God. How often do churches get wrapped up in massive church building projects? Far too many Christians mistakenly think that the church building should be a central focal point in a church's budget and planning. Buildings are important, but they ultimately pale in comparison to God's people as His ultimate building program. What might the global missions scene look like if, instead of building a bigger building to accommodate more people, large churches planted a new church or funded foreign missionaries? Having a church building is not wrong, but buildings can, and often do, turn into idols. As the church, we should always have an eye to planting new churches and sending missionaries into the field to build the Church of God, letting nothing obstruct the important work of evangelism to the nations.

I hope that the more we continue to study and read what Paul has written to the Galatian churches, the more we will understand the depths of the gospel. I hope that we will also pray that God would fill us with faith that we might look to Christ alone for our salvation and not try to merit God's favor through our obedience. And I hope that we will pray fervently that the gospel would continue to go forth into the nations, gathering together the true Israel, the people of God, those who look to Christ by faith alone. Ministers should also be encouraged by Paul's words, because through their preaching God is building his Church. As Caspar Olevianus, a sixteenth-century Reformer, writes, "No minister labors in vain, even if the whole world says he does. The gospel always bears fruit, which God wants to be revealed in individual sermons, by which some come to salvation and others end up testifying to their own wickedness."[1]

1. Gerald L. Bray, ed., *Galatians, Ephesians*, vol. 10, *Reformation Commentary on Scripture, New Testament* (Downers Grove, IL: IVP Academic, 2011), 50.

4

Justified by Faith Alone

GALATIANS 2:11–21

We ourselves are Jews by birth and not Gentile sinners;
yet we know that a person is not justified by works of the
law but through faith in Jesus Christ, so we also have
believed in Christ Jesus, in order to be justified by faith
in Christ and not by works of the law, because by works
of the law no one will be justified.

Over the last several sections, Paul has established that his commission issued directly from Christ, and not from or through man. This placed Paul's authority and commission equal to that of the original eleven apostles. Paul also explained that the same Holy Spirit that empowered James, Peter, and John to bring the gospel to the Jews empowered Paul to bring the gospel to the Gentiles. What was the message of the gospel? The bottom line is that a person is justified before God, not on account of his obedience to the law, but by believing in Jesus Christ. Justification, therefore, is by faith, not by works.

31

This was the gospel that the Galatian churches had initially embraced and accepted, but now, through the influence of false teachers, were rejecting. They had embraced the idea that one was saved by faith in Christ *and* through obedience to the law, which in this particular case meant submitting to circumcision. Paul countered that to follow this false gospel was to forfeit the freedom from the curse of the law that Christ had earned for them. In the passage before us, we see that even the apostle Peter was swept up to a certain degree by this false teaching, and Paul continues to drive a wedge between the two ways of justification. Either a person is justified by his own obedience to the law, which is an impossible path obstructed by sin and the curse of the law, or else a person looks by faith alone to Jesus Christ for justification.

Paul Confronts Peter

Peter was, at first, willing to sit down and share a meal with Gentile fellow Christians. Now, this might not seem like anything all that significant to us—what major problem is there in sharing a meal with a friend? Yet, we must remember that Jews and Gentiles would never have shared a meal, for at least two reasons.

First, Jews considered Gentiles ceremonially unclean. This is evident from Paul's characterization of Gentiles as "sinners" in verse 15. We might feel some apprehension about sitting down to dine with a known criminal, and a similar sentiment likely beset the average first-century Jew concerning Gentiles. Indeed, if you recall Christ's interaction with the Canaanite woman who had a demon-possessed daughter, Christ referred to her as a "dog" (Matt. 15:26–27).

Second, Gentiles were deemed unclean because they ate unclean foods. The Old Testament ceremonial law identified certain foods as unclean for Israelites; for instance, crustaceans

Justified by Faith Alone

(lobsters, crabs, and shrimp) and pork in all its forms were unclean (Lev. 11). So for these two reasons, the average Jew would have had significant obstacles to overcome before he would eat with a Gentile.

With the advent of Christ, these distinctions were swept away: "For he himself is our peace, who has made us both one and has broken down in his flesh the dividing wall of hostility by abolishing the law of commandments and ordinances, that he might create in himself one new man in place of the two" (Eph. 2:14–15). The abrogated status of these food laws was personally impressed upon Peter when he was atop the house of Simon the tanner. God lowered a sheet filled with all kinds of four-footed creatures, reptiles, and birds of the air. Peter knew that these animals were unclean—he practiced the food laws of Leviticus 11. Nevertheless, God told Peter: "Rise, Peter. Kill and eat. . . . What God has made clean, do not call common" (Acts 10:15). This is why Peter, at least initially, was willing to eat with Gentile Christians. But as soon as the circumcision party arrived in Antioch, Peter changed his conduct in a dramatic way.

The circumcision party was of the opinion that Gentiles had to be circumcised and accept the Jewish ceremonial laws in order to be saved. When these false teachers arrived at Antioch, Peter reversed course and refused to eat with his Gentile brothers in Christ. Moreover, Paul writes that Peter acted hypocritically (Gal. 2:13), which means he tried to minimize the nature of his fellowship with the Gentiles in an attempt to save face with the circumcision party. Peter's actions here are eerily reminiscent of his betrayal of Christ (Luke 22:54–61). When the servant girl of the high priest confronted Peter, he denied that he knew Christ. Similarly, when the circumcision party confronted Peter about his meals with Gentiles, he hypocritically withdrew and claimed to have nothing to do with them. Additionally, it seems the circumcision party demanded that the Gentiles submit to the ceremonial law and be circumcised. For this sinful conduct, Paul tells the Galatians that he "opposed Peter to his face" (v. 11).

Paul writes that Peter's conduct was sinful and betrayed the freedom that Christ had secured and therefore he "stood condemned" (v. 11). Paul asked Peter how he could live like a Gentile by eating with his Gentile brothers in Christ, and then demand that they become Jews by submitting to circumcision. Paul goes on to explain in greater detail the nature of the gospel so that the Galatians could grasp the enormity of Peter's error. Before we proceed, however, we should note the importance of our commitment to Christ even in the face of influential people.

Often, Christians will fail to stand for the truth of the gospel because they do not want to lose the approval of the wealthy or powerful. In other circumstances, we do not want to disrupt relationships and so we will compromise on the gospel instead of confronting friends or family. Paul's confrontation of Peter tells us that, no matter who the person is—friend, family, or foe— and no matter how influential one might be, our allegiance must always be to Christ and his gospel.

The Nature of the Gospel

Paul was willing to adopt the circumcision party's characterization of the Gentiles (as "sinners") to make his point regarding the nature of the gospel:

> We ourselves are Jews by birth and not Gentile sinners; yet we know that a person is not justified by works of the law but through faith in Jesus Christ, so we also have believed in Christ Jesus, in order to be justified by faith in Christ and not by works of the law, because by works of the law no one will be justified. (Galatians 2:15–16)

Justified by Faith Alone

Paul characterizes Gentiles as sinners, but he implicitly indicts Jews as well, since, as he explains, no one—Jew or Gentile—can be justified by works of the law.

In other words, not a single Jew or Gentile could be declared righteous by obedience to the law. Paul draws from the Old Testament to make his point: "And enter not into judgment with thy servant: for in thy sight shall no man living be justified" (Ps. 143:2, KJV). In its original context, David is appealing to God's faithfulness and righteousness, knowing that no one can stand in God's sight and be justified, since all flesh, whether Jew or Gentile, is worthy of God's condemnation.[1] Along these lines, John Calvin (1509–1564) writes:

> If David found refuge nowhere else than in prayer for pardon, who is there amongst us who would presume to come before God trusting in his own righteousness and integrity? Nor does David here merely set an example before God's people how they ought to pray, but declares that there is none amongst men who could be just before God were he called to plead his cause. The passage is one fraught with much instruction, teaching us, as I have just hinted, that God can only show favor to us in our approaches by throwing aside the character of a judge, and reconciling us to himself in a gratuitous remission of our sins. All human righteousness, accordingly, go for nothing, when we come to his tribunal.[2]

Paul makes explicit what is implicit in David's appeal, namely, that no one will be justified in God's sight on the basis of their obedience to the law. Or in this particular case, circumcision

---

1. Hans-Joachim Kraus, *Psalms 60–150* (Minneapolis, MN: Fortress, 1993), 536.

2. John Calvin, *Psalms 93–150*, vol. 6, *Calvin's Commentaries*, CTS (Grand Rapids, MI: Baker, 1993), 249.

cannot make a person righteous in God's sight.[3] If we cannot be justified by our obedience, then how can we escape God's wrath and judgment?

The answer comes in the gospel—justification by faith alone: "We know that a person is not justified by works of the law but through faith in Jesus Christ, so we also have believed in Christ Jesus, in order to be justified by faith in Christ and not by works of the law" (Gal. 2:16). Paul then brings the truth of the gospel to bear upon his confrontation with Peter: "But if, in our endeavor to be justified in Christ, we too were found to be sinners, is Christ then a servant of sin? Certainly not! For if I rebuild what I tore down, I prove myself to be a transgressor" (Gal. 2:17–18). In verse 17, Paul refutes the charge that he and the apostles were "sinners" in regard to circumcision (in the same way that Gentiles were before the New Covenant). Paul and the apostles had let go of circumcision in order to take hold of Christ in its place, so any attempt to recover circumcision was, by necessity, an attempt to displace Christ. Paul says that what has been torn down cannot be rebuilt. But what exactly has been torn down?

Remember, Paul had been zealously devoted to the traditions of his fathers (Gal. 1:14), but he had torn down this devotion and could not rebuild it. Why? Something was already in its place. If he were to rededicate himself to justification through the law, *then* he would be a transgressor. Why? Because the law demands absolute perfect obedience and brings a curse upon the one who tries to be justified by it. Christ came on behalf of *sinners* such as Paul and the Gentiles. He rendered his perfect obedience to the law, but nevertheless suffered its curse on behalf of the people of God. This is why

---

3. Moisés Silva, "Galatians," in *Commentary on the New Testament Use of the Old Testament*, eds. G. K. Beale and D. A. Carson (Grand Rapids, MI: Baker, 2007), 791.

Paul writes: "For through the law I died to the law, so that I might live to God. I have been crucified with Christ. It is no longer I who live, but Christ who lives in me. And the life I now live in the flesh I live by faith in the Son of God, who loved me and gave himself for me" (Gal. 2:19–20).

By faith, the believer is united to Christ; everything that belongs to Christ is transferred to the believer, and everything that belonged to the believer is transferred to Christ. In this regard, the death of Christ, his crucifixion, becomes the death of the believer. Therefore, through the death of Christ, the believer is freed from the demands and curse of the law. This is why Paul says that he was crucified with Christ. However, notice how Paul goes on to say that Christ now lives in him. In other words, it was the indwelling power of the Holy Spirit that enabled Paul to live by faith in Christ, not his own efforts to merit justification by obedience.

Paul drives his point home by stating the logical outcome of the Galatian heresy: "I do not nullify the grace of God, for if justification were through the law, then Christ died for no purpose" (Gal. 2:21). If the believer's justification is based upon the work of Christ and the obedience of the believer, then Christ came in vain. In other words, the work of Christ is insufficient to save and requires augmentation—the addition of the believer's obedience. If the false teachers are correct, then Christ did not secure salvation for anyone, but only the *possibility* or *opportunity* for salvation to those willing to complete their salvation with their own good works. This, however, is the farthest thing from the truth. This is why Paul calls the Galatian heresy a false gospel. Christ did not come to give people the possibility or the chance at salvation; he came to save his people from the wrath of God: actually, finally, completely, eternally, and immutably.

Modern False Gospels

Compromising the integrity of the gospel is nothing new. If Paul faced challenges from the Apostle Peter, one of the foundation stones of the church, then we should not be surprised when we face similar challenges in our own day. While the Galatian heresy specifically centered on issues related to the ceremonial law (food laws and circumcision), the manifestations of the false gospel in subsequent history have typically been a bit more generic: people have tried over the centuries to emphasize a general obedience to the "Law" rather than a specific aspect of the law, such as circumcision.

But there are those, who, similar to the Galatian Judaizers, have argued that the sign of the covenant (in our case, baptism) is necessary for a person's salvation. Most famously, of course, is the Roman Catholic doctrine that a believer is justified in his baptism and then by his own good works becomes even more justified.[4] The Galatian heresy, however, is not limited to the Roman Catholic Church. A proponent of the so-called Federal Vision has offered an explanation of justification that is strikingly similar to Roman Catholic views:

> God, not man, makes the water used in baptism. The one baptized has no works to offer. He is completely passive. But to do the Lord's Supper man must "make" bread and wine out of the raw materials of creation. The elements of the Supper represent human labor and are offered to God as a sacrifice of praise and thanks. Man is active in eating and drinking at the table, and God judges us according to our "works" therein (1 Cor 11:17ff). So baptism, as the sacrament of initiation, grants initial justification apart from works. But the Supper, as the sacrament

---

4. See "Canons and Decrees of the Council of Trent," session 6, chp. 7 in Philip Schaff, *Creeds of Christendom*, 3 vols. (1931; Grand Rapids, MI: Baker, 1990), II:94–97.

Justified by Faith Alone

> of nourishment and maturation, includes an evalua-
> tion of our works.[5]

This statement implies that a person is *initially* justified apart from works and *finally* justified by his works. What of David's cry in Psalm 143:2? What of Paul's use of David's cry in Galatians 2:15–16? We do not transmute Christ's works with our good works in the hopes that our concoction will produce the gold of eternal life.

Along slightly different lines, how many Christians teach justification by psychology? "I am not guilty of my sin because I have mental health issues." How many Christians believe in justification by remorse? "If I feel sorrier for my sin than an unrepentant sinner, then I'll be free from my guilt and sin." How many Christians believe in a layaway plan for their justification? "I can pay God back for my salvation if I can be obedient enough." No matter how well-intended these sentiments might be, like those of Peter, they stand condemned. Against all such muddled denials of the gospel, Paul's message is clear: "We know that a person is not justified by works of the law but through faith in Jesus Christ, so we also have believed in Christ Jesus, in order to be justified by faith in Christ and not by works of the law, because by works of the law no one will be justified" (Gal. 2:16).

The only proper response to the gospel is God-given faith in Christ. I close with the words of "Rock of Ages," written by Anglican pastor and hymn writer Augustus Toplady (1740–1778):

> Not the labors of my hands
> Can fulfill thy law's demands;
> Could my zeal no respite know,
> Could my tears forever flow,

---

5. Rich Lusk, "Response to Smith," in *The Auburn Avenue Theology: Pros and Cons. Debating the Federal Vision*, ed. E. Calvin Beisner (Ft. Lauderdale, FL: Knox Theological Seminary, 2004), 146 n. 73.

All for sin could not atone;
Thou must save, and thou alone.

Nothing in my hand I bring,
Simply to thy cross I cling;
Naked, come to thee for dress,
Helpless, look to thee for grace;
Foul, I to the Fountain fly;
Wash me, Savior, or I die.

5

Perfected by the Flesh?

GALATIANS 3:1–5

O foolish Galatians! Who has bewitched you? It was before your eyes that Jesus Christ was publicly portrayed as crucified. Let me ask you only this: Did you receive the Spirit by works of the law or by hearing with faith? Are you so foolish? Having begun by the Spirit, are you now being perfected by the flesh?

You've probably heard the phrase, "There's no such thing as a free lunch." How many times have you received a notice in the mail informing you that you have won a contest and all you have to do to claim your prize is make a phone call, buy something, or make a long-term commitment? The "contest" turns out to be a marketing ploy. In many cases, even if you actually do win a large sum of money or an automobile, you still have to pay hefty taxes on the prize. There is always some catch. Unfortunately, this reality has affected the thinking of many people within the church. They hear about the free message of the gospel and the forgiveness of sins—their free justification by faith alone in Christ alone by God's grace alone, and then, rather than relying upon the same power of the gospel for their lives as Christians, they think that they can somehow maintain their status by their good works. They think there is a hidden obligation—a catch—to the free gospel. This is the type of problem Paul confronted in the Galatian church.

In the passage before us, Paul continues to dissect and expose the problems with the Galatian heresy. And while Paul marshals an important theological point that pertains to justification—the place of entry into the Christian life—at the same time his teaching has important implications for our sanctification, the period of time after our initial conversion until either our death or the return of Christ. It is good to review what the Westminster Shorter Catechism has to say about justification and sanctification so we understand the difference between the two:

What is justification?

ANSWER: Justification is an act of God's free grace, wherein he pardoneth all our sins, and accepteth us as righteous in his sight, only for the righteousness of Christ imputed to us, and received by faith alone. (WSC 33)

What is sanctification?

ANSWER: Sanctification is the work of God's free grace, whereby we are renewed in the whole man after the image of God, and are enabled more and more to die unto sin, and live unto righteousness. (WSC 35)

Notice that justification and sanctification are equally of "God's free grace." However, justification is an *act*, a once-and-for-all event, whereas sanctification is a *work* of ongoing renovation.

Perfected by the Flesh?

Nothing can possibly add to the completed act of our justification, but we remain "works in progress" in terms of our sanctification. Keeping these things straight in our minds is important as we learn about the nature of both, and about living the Christian life.

You Foolish Galatians!

At the beginning of the chapter, Paul rebukes the Galatians for their foolish conduct and for embracing this false gospel. He asks, "Do you not understand that Jesus Christ was crucified on your behalf precisely to offer what was impossible for you to offer?" Paul's basic point forces the Galatians to ask the question, "Does our right standing before God depend upon the work of Christ crucified or does it depend on us?" The answer to this implied question comes in the verses that follow. Paul poses a question that places faith in Christ and works of the law in stark antithesis: "Let me ask you only this: Did you receive the Spirit by works of the law or by hearing with faith?" (Gal. 3:2). Paul asks this question because it is directly relevant regarding the place of works, or obedience to the law, in connection with our justification. Paul asks quite simply whether the Galatians received the Holy Spirit through their obedience to the law or through faith?[1] Or, if we narrow the nature of Paul's question to the specific issue confronting the Galatians, "Did you receive the Spirit by circumcision or by hearing through faith?" This

---

1. Contra New Perspective positions regarding the meaning of the phrase "works of the law." See N. T. Wright, *Paul: In Fresh Perspective* (Minneapolis, MN: Fortress, 2005), 54–55; James D. G. Dunn, *Jesus, Paul, and the Law* (Louisville, KY: Westminster John Knox Press, 1990), 194. The Reformers dismissed this type of explanation when Roman Catholic exegetes claimed the "works of the law" referred only to the ceremonial law. The New Perspective is thus not so new. See John Calvin, *Galatians, Ephesians, Philippians, and Colossians*, CNTC, trans. T. H. L. Parker, eds. David W. Torrance and T. F. Torrance (Grand Rapids, MI: Eerdmans, [1965] 1999), 66–67; Martin Luther, *Galatians*, vol. 26, *Luther's Works*, ed. Jaroslav Pelikan (St. Louis: Concordia, 1963), 122–123, 180–181.

question is a simple one but has profound implications for our understanding of justification.

When we place our faith in Jesus Christ, we are permanently and eternally inhabited by the Holy Spirit. Paul presses this point by asking the Galatians if they received the Holy Spirit through their obedience to the law. The implied answer is of course in the negative. No, they did not receive the Spirit by their obedience to the law. Why is this the case? Paul elsewhere explains that the law was never intended to justify a person: "For by works of the law no human being will be justified in his sight, since through the law comes knowledge of sin" (Rom. 3:20). Paul once again appeals to Psalm 143:2. The law reveals our sin, it shows us our unrighteousness, and identifies us as worthy of condemnation. Paul elaborates upon these themes in his first epistle to Corinth when he writes: "The sting of death is sin, and the power of sin is the law" (1 Cor. 15:56). The law, because of our sin, is powerless to save. Moreover, in connection with Paul's point, the law cannot impart the Holy Spirit.

Rather, the Spirit comes through the gospel, which comes through hearing the preaching of the Word. In other words, notice the contrast here—in the one, the assumption is that the Holy Spirit is obtained through effort, whereas in the other, the Holy Spirit is received through no effort on the part of the receiver. In his epistle to Rome, Paul explains how we receive the Holy Spirit: "For God has done what the law, weakened by the flesh, could not do. By sending his own Son in the likeness of sinful flesh and for sin, he condemned sin in the flesh, in order that the righteous requirement of the law might be fulfilled in us, who walk not according to the flesh but according to the Spirit" (Rom. 8:3–4). We do not receive the Holy Spirit through *our* obedience but rather by the obedience of Christ. We look to Christ by faith alone and receive the Holy Spirit as a gift.

Perfected by the Flesh?

Now, before we go forward, we should look back for a moment to the Old Testament and recall what it says regarding the outpouring of the Spirit: "And I will give you a new heart, and a new spirit I will put within you. And I will remove the heart of stone from your flesh and give you a heart of flesh. And I will put my Spirit within you, and cause you to walk in my statutes and be careful to obey my rules" (Ezek. 36:26–27). The prophet also states: "And I will put my Spirit within you, and you shall live, and I will place you in your own land. Then you shall know that I am the LORD; I have spoken, and I will do it, declares the LORD" (Ezek. 37:14). Or there is the famous statement by the prophet Joel: "And it shall come to pass afterward, that I will pour out my Spirit on all flesh" (Joel 2:28). In these Old Testament passages, the emphasis is on God as the one who will pour out his Spirit in spite of his people's disobedience. The outpouring of the Holy Spirit is a divine gift of God's mercy and love, not something that his people have earned the right to receive through their obedience.

In the verses that follow, Paul asks the Galatians several more questions that build off of this first question: "Are you so foolish? Having begun by the Spirit, are you now being perfected by the flesh" (Gal. 3:3)? These questions have implications for our understanding of both justification and sanctification. The Galatians would have answered in the negative to Paul's initial question: "Did you receive the Holy Spirit through your obedience?" The second question, slightly rephrased, is: "If you started by receiving God's grace in your justification, are you going to finish your redemption by your own obedience to the law?" Or, to put the question in the context of Paul's situation at Galatia: "If you started by faith in Christ, will you try to finish your redemption by your circumcision?" The answer to this question, regardless of how it may be posed, is no. As the author of Hebrews writes: Jesus is "the author *and* finisher of our faith"

(Heb. 12:2; emphasis added). Paul's broader point is that both justification and sanctification are by grace through faith alone in Christ by the power of the Holy Spirit. We are neither justified nor sanctified by our good works.

Charles Hodge (1797–1878), the famous theologian from Princeton Seminary, explains this important point:

> All that the Scriptures teach concerning the union between the believer and Christ, and of the indwelling of the Holy Spirit, proves the supernatural character of our sanctification. Men do not make themselves holy; their holiness, and their growth in grace, are not due to their own fidelity, or firmness or purpose, or watchfulness and diligence, although all these are required, but to the divine influence by which they are rendered thus faithful, watchful, and diligent, and which produces in them the fruits of righteousness.[2]

By all means, we as Christians are supposed to work out our salvation with fear and trembling, as Paul writes (Phil. 2:12). However, we must always realize that the source of our sanctity and holiness is Christ and his gospel, not our own efforts.

Moving forward, Paul asks the Galatians two more questions: "Did you suffer so many things in vain—if indeed it was in vain? Does he who supplies the Spirit to you and works miracles among you do so by works of the law, or by hearing with faith" (Gal. 3:4–5). Paul asks whether everything the Galatians have suffered on account of the gospel has been in vain. In the first century, Christians suffered great persecution on account of their faith and devotion to Christ. Paul's point raises the specter, however, of suffering for something else other than the gospel. To suffer for the gospel is a good thing, but to suffer for a false

---

2. Charles Hodge, *Systematic Theology*, 3 vols. (rep.; Grand Rapids, MI: Eerdmans, 1991), III:218.

gospel is to suffer in vain. He presses his point even further by asking whether it was their obedience to the law that caused God to work miracles in their midst, or whether they received the gospel, and its miraculous power, by faith in Christ. Again, the obvious answer to this question is that they have received the blessings of the Holy Spirit by faith, not through obedience.

When we stop to consider what Paul has written, there are at least two things to consider: the gospel is *free* and the entirety of our redemption is by grace alone through faith alone in Christ alone.

The Free Nature of the Gospel

One of the hardest things many Christians struggle with is the free nature of the gospel. We are conditioned by that old cliché that there is no free lunch. Consequently we think that there must be *something* that we do to contribute to our salvation—some act of obedience, some amount of righteousness, or some sort of effort that we must make. Yet manifestly in this passage, Paul constantly contrasts the works of the law (human effort) with the free gift of the Holy Spirit, which comes through faith. Martin Luther explains the contrast Paul is drawing:

> The Law never brings the Holy Spirit; therefore it does not justify, because it only teaches what we ought to do. But the Gospel does bring the Holy Spirit, because it teaches what we ought to receive. Therefore the Law and the Gospel are two altogether contrary doctrines. Accordingly, to put righteousness into the Law is simply to conflict with the Gospel. For the Law is a taskmaster; it demands that we work and that we give. In short, it wants to have something from us. The Gospel, on the contrary, does not demand; it grants freely; it commands us to hold out our hands and to receive what is being offered. Now demanding and granting, receiving and

offering, are exact opposites and cannot exist together. For that which is granted, I receive; but that
which I grant, I do not receive but offer to someone
else. Therefore if the Gospel is a gift and offers a gift,
it does not demand anything. On the other hand, the
Law does not grant anything; it makes demands on
us, and impossible ones at that.[3]

The gospel, our justification, and the indwelling presence of the
Holy Spirit are all free!

William Perkins (1558–1602), the famous sixteenth-century Puritan theologian, explains the relationship between law
and gospel in the following manner:

Here, I say, we see the difference between the law
and the gospel. The law does not minister the Spirit
to us: for it only shows our disease, and gives us no
remedy. The gospel ministers the Spirit. For it shows
what we are to do: and withal the Spirit is given, to
make us do that which we are enjoined in the gospel.[4]

God freely grants us the faith and enables us to believe, and,
when we believe, he freely forgives us of our sin, imputes to us
the righteousness of Christ, and his Holy Spirit permanently
indwells us.

Salvation Is by Grace Alone Through Faith Alone

The gift of our redemption is not incomplete. We likely all remember as children how some toys would be advertised with
the disclaimer, "batteries not included." Our redemption is not
one in which our sanctification is not included. Remember,
Christ is both the author and finisher of our faith—he who jus-

---

3. Martin Luther, *Galatians*, vol. 26, *Luther's Works*, ed. Jaroslav Pelikan (St.
Louis: Concordia Publishing House, 1963), 208–209.

4. William Perkins, *A Commentary on Galatians*, ed. Gerald T. Shepherd
(New York: Pilgrim Press, [1617] 1989), 144.

tifies us is also the one who sanctifies us through the work of the Holy Spirit. The language of the Shorter Catechism is helpful on this point: "Sanctification is the work of God's free grace, whereby we are renewed in the whole man after the image of God, and are enabled more and more to die unto sin, and live unto righteousness" (WSC 35). Our redemption is not some sort of 50/50 proposition—God provides his grace and then we give our best effort. Remember again what the prophet Ezekiel wrote: "And I will give you a new heart, and a new spirit I will put within you. And I will remove the heart of stone from your flesh and give you a heart of flesh. And I will put my Spirit within you, and cause you to walk in my statutes and be careful to obey my rules" (Ezek. 36:26–27).

We must yield, rest, and look by faith to Christ, and he conforms us to his image through the work of the Holy Spirit. As we will see later on in Paul's letter, the Holy Spirit produces his fruit in us. What is it that is supposed to mark our rest in Christ? We must draw near to him through the means of grace. In prayer, where we draw near to Christ and the Spirit, Jesus conforms us to his image. Through the reading and preaching of the Word, Christ conforms us to his image by the power of the Holy Spirit. These things are so simple, yet so many Christians fail to make use of the means of grace and thereby fail to draw near to Christ. We fail to pray. We do not read the Word. We fail to attend church to hear the preaching of the Word. Preachers fail to preach the Word. We avoid the sacraments or fail to make them a priority in our lives.

In this respect, Paul gives preachers important food for thought regarding their preaching ministry. Paul reminds the Galatians that Christ was "publicly portrayed as crucified" (Gal. 3:1). Calvin explains:

> Let those who want to discharge the ministry of the
> gospel aright learn not only to speak and declaim

but also to penetrate into consciences, so that men may see Christ crucified and that His blood may flow. When the Church has such painters as these she no longer needs wood and stone, that is, dead images, she no longer requires any pictures. And certainly images and pictures were first admitted to Christian temples when, partly, the pastors had become dumb and were mere shadows (*idola*), partly, when they uttered a few words from the pulpit so coldly and superficially that the power and efficacy of the ministry were utterly extinguished.[5]

Ultimately, ministers of the gospel herald the crucified Christ, not Jesus our "best friend," or our "co-pilot," or our "cosmic bell hop." In the end, preachers cannot offer any other substitutes, as only Christ justifies and sanctifies his people through the faithful preaching of the gospel.

There is nothing, absolutely nothing, that we can do to somehow curry God's favor. Instead, we must simply bask in God's unmerited favor: the mercy, love, and grace he has poured out upon us in Christ. The entirety of our redemption, including our justification and sanctification, is by God's grace. Therefore, rest in Christ. Seek the transforming power of the Spirit in the means of grace. Rejoice that Christ is both the author and finisher of our faith.

---

5. John Calvin, *Galatians, Ephesians, Philippians and Colossians*, CNTC (Grand Rapids, MI: Eerdmans, [1965] 1996), 47.

6

The Gospel in the Old Testament

GALATIANS 3:6–9

Know then that it is those of faith who are the sons of Abraham. And the Scripture, foreseeing that God would justify the Gentiles by faith, preached the gospel beforehand to Abraham, saying, "In you shall all the nations be blessed." So then, those who are of faith are blessed along with Abraham, the man of faith.

How old is the gospel? We live in a self-centered time where people do not have historical roots. Many people hardly know their own family trees and can trace their ancestors back only one, maybe two generations. The same mindset affects the church in that many situate the origins of the gospel in their own conversion, or perhaps they push it back to their parents, or if they really go back, they might date it to the "ancient" days of Billy Graham. In one sense, the false teachers at Galatia had a similar type of historical amnesia. They believed that the gospel had recent origins because, among other things, the earthly ministry of Jesus had just occurred about two decades earlier. However, Paul wanted the Galatians to know that the gospel was much older than the ministry of Christ. It stretched back to the Old Testament and the earliest days of redemptive history.

Paul therefore transitions from the Galatians' personal experience to the Old Testament to demonstrate that believers have always been justified by faith alone, and not by obedience. That Paul appeals to the Old Testament is important for at least two reasons. First, it shows his opponents that he is not at all out of step with the Scriptures—the Old Testament confirms his message. But second, it shows that God's redemptive plan and purpose have always been the same. God did not devise plan A with Israel and, when that did not work, switch to plan B with the Gentiles.[1] On the contrary, Paul explains that the gospel was preached from the earliest days of the Old Testament.

Imputation and Justification

For the sake of context, one should read the verse that immediately precedes verse 6: "Does he who supplies the Spirit to you and works miracles among you do so by works of the law, or by hearing with faith—just as Abraham 'believed God, and it was counted to him as righteousness?'" (Gal. 3:5–6). Paul segues from his question concerning how the Galatians received the gift of the Holy Spirit, whether it was by faith or works, to quoting Genesis 15:6. At the time, Abraham believed that he was going to give his belongings and inheritance to his servant, Eliezer of Damascus. The Lord had different plans, however. He met with Abraham, took him outside his tent, and showed him the stars of the sky: "And he brought him outside and said, 'Look toward heaven, and number the stars, if you are able to number them.' Then he said to him, 'So shall your offspring be'"

---

1. Contra Dispensationalism; see, e.g., Charles Ryrie, *Dispensationalism Today* (1965; Chicago: Moody Press, 1970), 132–155.

(Gen. 15:5). God gave Abraham a promise, a promise that his offspring would be as numerous as the stars in the sky.

How did Abraham respond to God's promise? Genesis 15:6 states: "And he believed the LORD, and He counted it to him as righteousness." Notice why Paul appeals to this text. First, Abraham did not do anything in terms of fulfilling the requirements of the law. Abraham did not offer his obedience. Or more specifically, in relation to the Galatian heresy, Abraham was not yet circumcised. He is circumcised two chapters later in the narrative (Gen. 17), yet Paul notes that Abraham was accounted as righteous in God's sight. Abraham's righteous status came through faith—looking to the promise of God and believing that he would do what he said, namely, that God would give him offspring as numerous as the stars in the sky.

Second, Genesis 15:6 says that God "counted it to him as righteousness." How is it that Abraham was righteous in God's sight? Plainly and clearly, Abraham was not justified because of his works. Rather, God credited, or imputed, righteousness to Abraham's account: "And to the one who does not work but trusts in him who justifies the ungodly, his faith is counted as righteousness" (Rom. 4:5). Abraham had no righteousness of his own, yet he believed in the promise of God, and God credited Abraham with righteousness. What is righteousness? It is adherence to a moral-ethical standard.[2] If someone is perfectly obedient to the law, he is righteous—he has offered what the law demands. On the heels of God's re-administration of the Mosaic law, Israel understood the basic relationship between the law, its performance, and righteousness: "And it will be righteousness for us, if we are careful to do all this commandment before the LORD our God, as he has commanded us" (Deut.

---

2. Contra N. T. Wright, "Romans and the Theology of Paul," in *Pauline Theology*, ed. David M. Hay and E. Elizabeth Johnson (Minneapolis, MN: Fortress, 1995), III:38–39.

6:25). In a word, righteousness is moral equity. But here is the amazing thing about justification by faith alone—Abraham offered no obedience. Instead Abraham believed, and God looked at him as if he had offered perfect obedience to the law. Abraham is righteous, not by doing, but by believing; not by works, but by faith alone in Christ alone (cf. John 8:56).

The declaration of Abraham's righteousness in Genesis 15:6 is stunning, even breathtaking. Why? Because the whole Abrahamic narrative makes it clear that Abraham was *sinful*. We should not dismiss the fact that Abraham doubted God's faithfulness (Gen. 15:2–3). Abraham and Sarah sinfully concocted their own method to bring about God's promise, which involved using Sarah's handmaid, Hagar, as a surrogate wife (Gen. 16). Shortly after this, Abraham lied to King Abimelech and, fearing for his life, told him that Sarah was his sister. Abraham's deceitful conduct earned him a rebuke from an unbelieving pagan (Gen. 20:9). One could hardly characterize Abraham's actions as *righteous*. Yet, by faith alone, God declared Abraham righteous—that is, he declared him to be one who has met the demands of the law. The gospel brings the jaw-dropping mercy of God in Christ and justifies sinners who would otherwise be justly condemned. As Christ told the Pharisees, he came to save sinners, not the righteous (Mark 2:17).

True Sons of Abraham

If faith alone is the manner by which Abraham was justified and righteous in God's sight, then what are the implications for the Galatians? Certainly relevant is Paul's point that righteousness does not come through obedience to the law. Related to this is the question of who the true descendants of Abraham really are. The Judaizers at Galatia, those who insisted that the Gentiles be circumcised to be a part of the covenant, believed that in order to participate in the blessings of the Abrahamic covenant, a Gentile had to become a Jew. If reception of the covenant blessings is by faith alone, then this means that the Judaizers misunderstood the nature of the covenant. They believed that the Gentiles had to be circumcised so they could become an "offspring" of Abraham and, by consequence, a recipient of the covenant blessings. But what does Paul say in this regard? "Know then that it is those of faith who are the sons of Abraham" (Gal. 3:7). Here is the amazing thing: the people of God, the descendants of Abraham, are those who possess faith in Christ. The sons of Abraham are not physical descendants but spiritual descendants. This means that anyone, Jew or Gentile, can be a son of Abraham if he possesses faith in Christ.

The Gospel in the Old Testament

Paul's conclusion, however, is nothing new. As I intimated in the introduction, God did not scrap plan A and switch to plan B. Paul explains that the gospel—salvation by faith in the promise of God, which finds its fulfillment in Christ—has always been plan A: "And the Scripture, foreseeing that God would justify the Gentiles by faith, preached the gospel beforehand to Abraham, saying, 'In you shall all the nations be blessed'" (Gal. 3:8). Paul's statement is an important capstone to the message of the Scriptures, namely the universal scope and extent of the gospel.

First, Paul says that, in the promise God made to Abraham in Genesis 12:3, the personified Scriptures included the Gentiles in the redemptive plan of God. How do we know this? Genesis states: "I will bless those who bless you, and him who dishonors you I will curse, and in you all the families of the earth shall be blessed" (Gen. 12:3). The original promise, one that brought Abraham justification by faith alone, states that all of the families of the earth would be blessed (i.e., the blessing would extend globally). This encompasses all people, both Jews and Gentiles.

Second, take careful note of what Paul calls the promise in which Abraham placed his faith—the gospel. The gospel was preached in the Old Testament! Paul writes about this in Romans: "He will justify the circumcised by faith and the uncircumcised through faith" (Rom. 3:30). Now, to be sure, Paul is not setting forth a generic faith and playing fast and loose with what we know to be the gospel. In other words, we understand the gospel to denote believing and trusting in the person and work of Jesus Christ. Yet, how can Paul say that the gospel, believing in Christ, existed *prior* to Christ's advent? This is a question that Paul will answer in subsequent sections of his epistle.

Nevertheless, for the time being, it is helpful to look ahead to substantiate the claim that Abraham's faith was in Christ and not just a generic trust in God. In the verses that follow, Paul specifically states that Christ redeemed believers from the curse of the law and that the blessing of Abraham comes through Christ Jesus (Gal. 3:13–14). Paul then specifically identifies the recipient of the promises as Jesus: "Now the promises were made to Abraham and to his seed. It does not say, 'And to seeds,' referring to many, but referring to one, 'And to your seed,' who is Christ" (Gal. 3:16*). Paul was not propagating anything new, as Christ himself attested to the very point that Paul raises: "Your father Abraham rejoiced that he would see my day. He saw it and was glad" (John 8:56). So, then, according to Paul's explanation, the gospel of Jesus Christ was operative in the Old Testament.

Before we move forward, however, we should reflect for a few moments on the nature of the blessings that came to Abraham. The promise of God was that, in Abraham, all of the nations would be blessed, both Jew and Gentile. What is the nature of the blessing? The shortest answer comes from the Aaronic blessing: "The LORD bless you and keep you; the LORD make his face to shine upon you and be gracious to you;

the Lord lift up his countenance upon you and give you peace" (Num. 24:24–26). The blessing of the Abrahamic covenant, of the gospel, is one that involves the protection and nurture of almighty God. It brings with it the unmerited favor of God. It brings peace with God. If we are sinners and liable to God's just and holy condemnation, suffering his eternal wrath, then we are not at peace with God. But if a person looks to Christ by faith and trusts in the promise, then the blessing of Abraham is poured out on him. He now has peace with God—he no longer knows God as Judge, but as Father. This is why Paul writes in verse 9: "So then, those who are of faith are blessed along with Abraham, the man of faith" (Gal. 3:9).

One Plan for the Ages

Some who call themselves Christian theologians would dare to describe God as one who is capricious or one who is likely to change his mind about his plans.[3] Indeed, many well-intentioned, conservative Christians believe that God changed the plan of salvation. In the Old Testament, it is frequently said, God saved Israel by their obedience to the law and their sacrifices, but in the New Testament, he now saves people by his grace through Christ.[4] Such an opinion, no matter how sincerely held, is false and at odds with what Paul has written here.

From the very outset of creation, it was God's intention to fill the earth with people who bore his image and worshipped him. This is the import of the dominion mandate given to the first Adam: be fruitful, multiply, fill the earth, and subdue it.[5] But Adam sinned and forfeited his right to rule over the cre-

---

3. See Richard Rice et al., eds., *The Openness of God: A Biblical Challenge to the Traditional Understanding* (Downers Grove, IL: InterVarsity Press, 1994).

4. Cf. Charles C. Ryrie, *Dispensationalism: Revised and Expanded* (Chicago: Moody, [1966] 2007), 121–142.

5. See G. K. Beale, *The Temple and the Church's Mission: A Biblical Theology of the Dwelling Place of God*, NSBT (Downers Grove, IL: IVP Academic, 2004).

ation as God's vice-regent and brought sin and death into the world. In the face of man's rebellion, God promised that the seed of the woman would crush the head of the serpent and deliver God's people from their fallen state. Paul has explained that it is through Abraham's seed that all of the families of the earth would be blessed. And now, it is by trusting that seed, by trusting in the Lord Jesus Christ, as did Abraham thousands of years ago, that both Jew and Gentile are saved.

Despite Paul's crystal clarity in this text, people in the broader church refuse to submit to the message of Scripture. Perhaps one of the most flagrant examples of this refusal to submit to the authority of Scripture comes from the Roman Catholic Church. In an official document from Vatican II entitled, "Light of the Nations" (*Lumen Gentium*), we read:

> Nor is God remote from those who in shadows and
> images seek the unknown God, since he gives to ev-
> eryone life and breath and all things (see Acts 17:25–
> 28) and since the Savior wills everyone to be saved
> (see 1 Tim 2:4). Those who, through no fault of their
> own, do not know the Gospel of Christ or his church,
> but who nevertheless seek God with a sincere heart,
> and, moved by grace, try in their actions to do his
> will as they know it through the dictates of their con-
> science—these too may attain eternal salvation. Nor
> will divine providence deny the assistance necessary
> for salvation to those who, without any fault of theirs,
> have not yet arrived at an explicit knowledge of God,
> and who, not without grace, strive to lead a good life.
> Whatever of good or truth is found amongst them is
> considered by the Church to be a preparation for the
> Gospel and given by him who enlightens all men and
> women that they may at length have life.[6]

---

6. *Lumen Gentium*, §16, in *The Basic Sixteen Documents of Vatican Council II: Constitutions, Decrees, Declarations*, ed. Austin Flannery, OP (Northport, NY: Costello Publishing Co., 1996), 221–222.

The Gospel in the Old Testament

Here Rome states that a person, apart from the gospel, can be saved if he lives an upright life. If this were not bad enough, the document goes on to claim: "The plan of salvation also includes those who acknowledge the Creator, first among whom are the Muslims: they profess to hold the faith of Abraham, and together with us they adore the one, merciful God, who will judge humanity on the last day."[7]

The Roman Catholic Church thus makes the absurd claim that Muslims share the faith of Abraham. Such an assertion is without the slightest shred of biblical support. According to Paul, Abraham looked to Jesus by faith alone. Jesus also said as much (John 8:56–58). Beyond that, we have in Romans 10:13–17 the categorical denial of any possibility of salvation for those who follow other religions. In our day, however, the exclusivity of the Christian gospel is under constant attack by those who have capitulated to the pluralistic spirit of the age. Such claims, of which this Roman Catholic pronouncement is but one example, stand in total antithesis to the claims of Paul; we can be certain that Abraham and Muslims in no way share the same faith.

God has never changed his mind; he has been faithful throughout the ages to his one promise, the promise of the gospel. If salvation has always been by grace alone through faith alone in Christ alone, even in the days of Abraham, then we as the church—the herald of the gospel—must continue to proclaim this message to the nations. We must herald that message to both Jew and Gentile, to American and Arab, to the Chinese and Japanese, and tell the world that anyone can become a child of Abraham by placing his faith in Christ. In so doing, anyone, Jew or Gentile, can receive the blessing of Abraham and know God as Father and not Judge. Any person through faith alone in Christ alone can receive the blessing: the presence of God, his guiding, all-caring hand of protection, the glory and beauty of

---

7. *Lumen Gentium*, §16, in *Documents of Vatican II*, 221–222.

beholding his face, and his peace. As we carry this message into the world, we should look back in hope, knowing that God has been faithful throughout the ages to his promise of the gospel. We should not look to the world for hope, nor to our friends, nor to our families, but to our faithful heavenly Father—the one who justifies the ungodly through faith alone and credits the righteousness of his Son to anyone who believes in him.

So, then, the gospel is not a new or recent thing. It is not something that began in the New Testament with Christ and his disciples. We should realize how far back the gospel stretches. In terms of Paul's letter to the Galatians, he tells them that the gospel stretches all the way back to Abraham. In terms of our study of what Paul has said, the gospel reaches all the way back to the Garden of Eden when God promised that the seed of the woman would crush the head of the serpent (Gen. 3:15). Therefore, dear Christian, rejoice in knowing that it is by faith in Jesus Christ that we are saved. Long for the day when Christ will return, when people from every tribe, tongue, and nation will gather around the throne and worship the Lamb who was slain (Rev. 5:9–14).

7

The Righteous Shall Live by Faith Alone

GALATIANS 3:10–14

For all who rely on works of the law are under a curse; for it is written, "Cursed be everyone who does not abide by all things written in the Book of the Law, and do them." Now it is evident that no one is justified before God by the law, for "The righteous shall live by faith." But the law is not of faith, rather "The one who does them shall live by them." Christ redeemed us from the curse of the law by becoming a curse for us—for it is written, "Cursed is everyone who is hanged on a tree"— so that in Christ Jesus the blessing of Abraham might come to the Gentiles, so that we might receive the promised Spirit through faith.

Over the last two chapters, we have glanced into the heart of Paul's theological arguments to refute the heresy that had infected the Galatian churches. The Galatians embraced the idea that they were justified by both faith in Christ and by their obedience to the law, specifically, that one had to be circumcised. The Judaizers were teaching that Gentiles had to become Jews in order to be saved and therefore required that they be circumcised. Paul has pointed out from the outset that this understanding is a false gospel and has repeatedly emphasized that a person is not justified by his obedience but by faith alone in Christ alone. Paul has also drawn from the Old Testament to show that it was God's intention from the very outset to create a people for himself comprising both Jews and Gentiles. Now, he continues to expound the nature of the gospel and the doctrine of justification in the verses before us. These verses are very densely packed. Though we are examining a mere five verses, Paul nevertheless quotes four different passages from the Old Testament and alludes to at least another four Old Testament passages. This section is a tightly coiled spring of information, but if we carefully unpack it, we will have a greater understanding of the gospel and of the person and work of Christ.

The Function of the Law

Paul begins this section of chapter three by marshalling more evidence from the Old Testament to support the point that salvation is by faith alone and not by works. In the section preceding verse 10, he cited Genesis 15:6, "Abraham believed God and it was counted to him as righteousness," to show that salvation is by faith alone in Christ alone by God's grace alone. In verse 10, Paul cites the Old Testament to show the flipside of the coin: if salvation is by faith alone, what happens if a person tries to secure his salvation through his obedience to the law? The apostle writes: "For all who rely on works of the law are under a curse; for it is written, 'Cursed be everyone who does not abide by all things written in the Book of the Law, and do them'" (Gal. 3:10).

Paul quotes Deuteronomy 27:26 to show that if a person tries to bring forth his obedience to the law as the ground for his salvation, the only thing he will secure for himself is a curse. In its original context, Deuteronomy 27 came towards the end of the renewal of the Mosaic covenant before the people entered the Promised Land. God told them through Moses that if they were disobedient to the law, then they would merit the curses of the covenant. Israel was bound, not just to certain portions of the law, but to "abide by all things written in the book of the law, and do them." And to violate one part of the law was to violate the whole law (James 2:10). This is why Paul confidently states that those who rely on works of the law, or their obedience, are under a curse.

Although the Mosaic law in its fullness pointed to Christ, the law by itself was never intended to be a means of salvation. It is the mirror into which we look to identify our sinfulness—to show us how short we fall. Paul makes this point and then states that salvation is by faith alone and not by works: "Now it is evident that no one is justified before God by the law, for 'The righteous shall live by faith'" (Gal. 3:11). Here in verse 11, Paul quotes a second passage from the Old Testament: Habakkuk 2:4. In the original context, Habakkuk complained bitterly to the Lord that Israel was no longer a holy nation. Though they had once stood at the threshold of the Promised Land and vowed obedience to the law, the Israelites had since abandoned their commitment and were living wickedly. God had already carried the northern kingdom of Israel off into captivity, and now the threat of a Babylonian invasion and captivity were looming on the horizon for the southern kingdom of Judah as well.

The answer to Habakkuk's complaint was not that Israel should re-double her efforts and renew her obedience to the law to avert a Babylonian invasion. Rather, the faithful remnant in the southern kingdom of Judah had to live by faith—faith in the covenant promises of the Lord.[1] Hence, Paul appeals to

---

1. F. F. Bruce, *Habakkuk*, in *The Minor Prophets: An Exegetical and Expository Commentary*, 3 vols., ed. Thomas Edward McComiskey (Grand Rapids, MI: Baker, 1999), II:860–861.

Habakkuk 2:4 to make his point—salvation comes not through obedience but through faith, faith in Christ. Paul then places faith and works in complete and total antithesis to one another in the following verse: "But the law is not of faith, rather 'The one who does them shall live by them'" (Gal. 3:12). The apostle then offers a third quotation from the Old Testament. Leviticus 18:5 comes out of the application of the Mosaic covenant to the life of Israel and states quite simply the principle of the law—if you obey, you live, if you disobey, you die.[2] Machen explains Paul's point:

> These words, "he who has done them shall live in them," Paul means to say, "describe the nature of the law." It requires *doing* something. But faith is the opposite of doing. So when the Scripture says that a man is justified by faith, that involves saying that he is *not* justified by anything that he does. There are two conceivable ways of salvation. One way is to keep the law perfectly, to *do* the things which the law requires. No mere man since the fall has accomplished that. The other way is to *receive* something, to receive something that is freely given by God's grace. That way is followed when a man has faith. But you cannot possibly mingle the two. You might conceivably be saved by works or you might be saved by faith; but you cannot be saved by both. It is "either or" here not "both and." But which shall it be, works or faith? The Scripture gives the answer. The Scripture says it is faith. Therefore it is *not* works.[3]

---

2. See Bryan Estelle, "Leviticus 18:5 and Deuteronomy 30:1–14 in Biblical Theological Development: Entitlement to Heaven Foreclosed and Proffered," in *The Law Is Not of Faith: Essays on Grace and Works in the Mosaic Covenant*, eds. Bryan Estelle, J. V. Fesko, and David VanDrunen (Phillipsburg, NJ: P&R, 2008), 109–146.

3. J. Gresham Machen, *Notes on Galatians*, ed. John H. Skilton (Philadelphia: Presbyterian and Reformed, 1972), 178.

The Righteous Shall Live by Faith Alone

As Paul already pointed out, anyone who tries to pursue obedience to the law has an insurmountable obstacle standing in his way—sin. This means that all people are under the curse of the law. Does this mean, then, that we are without hope? By no means!

Paul moves forward to explain how the work of Christ relates to the curse of the law: "Christ redeemed us from the curse of the law by becoming a curse for us—for it is written, 'Cursed is everyone who is hanged on a tree'" (Gal. 3:13). In this verse, he offers a fourth quotation from the Old Testament, specifically, Deuteronomy 21:23. In its original context, this passage described a fitting punishment for a truly odious covenant breaker, one who had violated the law to such a degree that his punishment needed to serve as a warning to others. The covenant breaker was put to death, perhaps by stoning, and then his body was hung on a tree for no longer than the rest of the day. This action demonstrated God's curse on the covenant-breaker.[4] So even though the people of Israel, both individually and corporately, had forfeited their rights to reward for their obedience and instead had merited only God's wrath and curse, Christ redeemed them out from under the curse of God by becoming a curse for them. In Christ's crucifixion, he suffered the curses of the covenant on behalf of the people of God. But to what end did Christ suffer?

We immediately know that Christ suffered to remove the curse of the law from those who look to him by faith. Specifically, he "redeemed" (*exagorazo*) God's people, writes Paul. This is the same language that God used in describing his deliverance of Israel from its bondage in Egypt (cf. Gal. 4:5).[5] In other words, God's people were under the power of Satan, sin, death,

4. Peter C. Craigie, *The Book of Deuteronomy*, NICOT (Grand Rapids, MI: Eerdmans, 1976), 285–286.

5. Thomas Schreiner, *Galatians*, ZECNT (Grand Rapids, MI: Zondervan, 2010), 216.

and the curse of the law, but God freed them through Christ. Beyond that, Paul also writes: "Christ redeemed us from the curse of the law by becoming a curse for us—for it is written, 'Cursed is everyone who is hanged on a tree'—so that in Christ Jesus the blessing of Abraham might come to the Gentiles, so that we might receive the promised Spirit through faith" (Gal. 3:13–14). Through his obedience and suffering, Christ secured the promise and blessing of the Abrahamic covenant.

In verse 14, Paul alludes to at least four more different Old Testament passages. He refers to Genesis 12:3 and God's promise to give Abraham innumerable descendants. Then, notice how Paul writes that Christ's work brings the outpouring of the Holy Spirit. There are a number of passages in the Old Testament where God promised he would pour out his Spirit on all flesh, both Jew and Gentile (Joel 2:28–29; Isa. 32:15; 44:3; Ezek. 39:29). Interestingly enough, these Old Testament passages indicate that the outpouring of the Spirit would come on the heels of God's judgment against Israel as they lay in exile. In other words, God fulfilled his promise to pour out his Spirit upon his people, but it came, not through their obedience, but in spite of their *disobedience.* The promise was realized because of God's faithfulness and because Christ fulfilled the obligations of the law—bearing the curse of the covenant and securing redemption for the people of God.

By Faith Alone

Paul is emphatic about the importance of faith. In chapter three, he uses the word *faith* fifteen times—nine times in verses 1–14 alone. The apostle is absolutely insistent about impressing upon his readers the centrality of faith to salvation and erasing the Galatians' reliance upon their own works and obedience. We might perhaps think that such an insistence was necessary in Paul's day but not in our own. Surely people in the church know that salvation is by God's grace alone by faith alone in Christ alone, right? Unfortunately, this is not at all the case. In a recent Barna poll, forty-six percent of professing Christians surveyed agreed with the following statement: "If a person is generally good, or does enough good things for others during their life, they will earn a place in heaven."[6] Agreement with this statement is in fact worse than the Galatian heresy. At least in Galatia they believed that faith in Christ was necessary, though they erroneously added their own obedience to the work of Christ. In this question, however, there is no mention of Christ! Here, nearly half of those surveyed are under the impression that they do not need Christ whatsoever, but that they can secure their salvation without him.

We all have a tendency to think that our obedience will somehow be enough to satisfy God's judgment. We believe that we have been given the law as a ladder so that we can somehow, perhaps even with a little of God's grace, scale the heights of heaven and at last reach its gates. We do not realize that no matter how hard we try, we will always fall short. We are sinful, not only because of our own personal sins, but also because of the sin of Adam, our first father—his sin and guilt has been credited to our account (Rom. 5:12–19). With the sin of Adam added to our own personal sin, rendering perfect obedience to the law is about as feasible as swimming from California to Hawaii with a truck tied to our neck. Such a feat is, obviously, utterly and totally impossible.

The law has not been given to us so we can justify ourselves before God, or win his favor. No. The law has been given to expose our sin—we lie under its curse and are therefore liable to God's just wrath and condemnation. As William Perkins explains:

---

6. Barna Group, "What Americans Believe About Universalism and Pluralism," 18 April 2011, http://www.barna.org/faith-spirituality/484-what-americans-believe-about-universalism-and-pluralism (accessed 20 July 2011).

> When Paul says, "the law is not of faith" he sets down the main difference between the law and the gospel. The law promises life, to him that performs perfect obedience, and that for his works. The gospel promises life, to him that does nothing in the cause of salvation, but only believes in Christ: and it promises salvation to him that believes, yet not for his faith, or for any works else, but for the merit of Christ. The law then requires the doing to salvation, and the gospel believing, and nothing else.[7]

Christ redeems us from the curse of the law and his perfect work requires nothing from us. The crediting of Christ's work to us resembles the bestowal of Isaac's blessing on Jacob (Gen. 27). Recall how Jacob desired the covenant blessing of his firstborn brother, Esau. He deceived Isaac by wearing Esau's coat (to smell and feel like him) so that he could receive his brother's covenant blessing. There are some similarities between Jacob's efforts and our own redemption. But there is also great dissimilarity.

We must appear before our heavenly father so that we can receive the blessing of our older firstborn brother, Jesus. But we do not have to try to deceive our heavenly father by stealing the coat of our older brother so that we smell and feel like him. On the contrary, Christ freely gives his coat of righteousness to anyone who looks to him by faith. And in exchange, Christ wears the garment of our sin, guilt, and shame. We wear his coat, and he wears ours. Christ bears the punishment, wrath, and covenant curse on our behalf, and we receive his perfect righteousness, obedience, and blessing. We receive this blessing through faith alone—trusting in the work of Christ; his obedience, not ours; his suffering, not ours. As John Calvin writes: "For in order that we may appear before God's face unto salvation we must smell sweetly with his odor, and our vices must be

---

7. William Perkins, *A Commentary on Galatians*, ed. Gerald T. Shepherd (New York: Pilgrim Press, [1617] 1989), 170.

covered and buried by his perfection."[8] We then stand freely in the presence of our heavenly father and receive the blessing due to our firstborn brother. We receive the blessing of Abraham and the promised outpouring of the Holy Spirit. This blessing comes through faith alone, not through our works.

The gospel is good news because Christ has secured our redemption. We should therefore rejoice! This is why Paul elsewhere cries out, "For I am sure that neither death nor life, nor angels nor rulers, nor things present nor things to come, nor powers, nor height nor depth, nor anything else in all creation, will be able to separate us from the love of God in Christ Jesus our Lord" (Rom. 8:38–39). Christ has not simply secured the possibility of our salvation, leaving us to try our best and then hope that God grades on a curve. No! That is the very kind of thinking that Paul condemns and labels as a false gospel. Look to Christ. Do not work to gain your redemption, but rest in His perfect work of redemption on your behalf. Look to him by faith alone and trust that he has redeemed you from the curse of the law.

8. John Calvin, *Institutes of the Christian Religion*, ed. John T. McNeill, trans. Ford Lewis Battles, vols. 20–21, *The Library of Christian Classics* (Philadelphia: The Westminster Press, 1960), XX:III.XI.23.

8

The Promised Seed

GALATIANS 3:15–18

Now the promises were made to Abraham and to his offspring. It does not say, "And to offsprings," referring to many, but referring to one, "And to your offspring," who is Christ. This is what I mean: the law, which came 430 years afterward, does not annul a covenant previously ratified by God, so as to make the promise void. For if the inheritance comes by the law, it no longer comes by promise; but God gave it to Abraham by a promise.

There are many well-intentioned brothers and sisters in Christ who believe that God has different plans of redemption for Israel and for the Gentiles.[1] Perhaps more popularly, people believe that God made a conditional agreement with Israel to save them—if, and only if, they obeyed. God was gracious to them but they had to make use of the sacrifices for the forgiveness of sin and they also had to offer their obedience. If they fell short, then they could not be saved. God's dealings

---

1. See Charles Ryrie, *Dispensationalism Today* (Chicago: Moody Press, [1965] 1970).

with the church, on the other hand, were totally on the basis of his grace. God purportedly saw that Israel was an utter failure and could not render their obedience and even rejected him, so he turned to the Gentiles and offered to save them *without* the condition of their obedience. Such a view of salvation in the Old Testament appears in the *Left Behind* series,[2] and, unfortunately, this erroneous view is quite common and widespread.

Paul, on the other hand, does not explain God's relationship to Israel in these terms. Moreover, the apostle under the divine inspiration of the Holy Spirit, infallibly and inerrantly explains that the covenant that God made to Abraham was not dependent upon Abraham's obedience to the Mosaic law. Rather, the covenant was dependent upon God and his promise, and was ultimately fulfilled in Christ. In other words, in terms of Paul's overarching argument, salvation is by faith alone in Christ alone.

To the One Seed

Remember what Paul has written in verses 10–14. He argued that all who rely on the works of the law (or their obedience) are under a curse. Justification and salvation cannot come through our obedience because of our sinfulness—not only the inherited guilt of our first parents, Adam and Eve, but also because of our own personal sins. To violate one part of the law is to violate the whole law. Paul made the point quite emphatically that Christ came and suffered the curse of the covenant on behalf of those who look to him by faith. In other words, salvation and justification are not dependent upon our obedience, or in Paul's specific refutation, upon circumcision, but solely upon faith.

Paul continues to make his point by elaborating on the nature of the Abrahamic covenant and explaining its relationship to the Mosaic covenant. He begins in verse 15 by writing: "To

---

2. Tim LaHaye and Jerry B. Jenkins, *Left Behind: A Novel of Earth's Last Days* (Carol Stream, IL: Tyndale House, 2011).

The Promised Seed

give a human example, brothers: even with a man-made covenant, no one annuls it or adds to it once it has been ratified" (Gal. 3:15). Paul draws an example from common practice that people can make an agreement, a contract, and the terms of that contract are inviolable and unchanging. In similar fashion, he explains that this is the nature of the covenant that God made with Abraham: "Now the promises were made to Abraham and to his seed. It does not say, 'And to seeds,' referring to many, but referring to one, 'And to your seed,' who is Christ" (Gal. 3:16*).

Paul explains that inviolable and unchanging covenantal promises were made to Abraham. The promises were made, however, not only to Abraham, but also to his descendants. We read the following in the Genesis narrative:

> After these things the word of the Lord came to Abram in a vision: "Fear not, Abram, I am your shield; your reward shall be very great." But Abram said, "O Lord God, what will you give me, for I continue childless, and the heir of my house is Eliezer of Damascus?" And Abram said, "Behold, you have given me no seed, and a member of my household will be my heir." And behold, the word of the Lord came to him: "This man shall not be your heir; your very own son shall be your heir." And he brought him outside and said, "Look toward heaven, and number the stars, if you are able to number them." Then he said to him, "So shall your seed be." (Genesis 15:1–5*)

Now, the immediate thing that should strike us is that Abraham's descendants, or his seed, will be as numerous as the stars in the sky. They will be innumerable. In other words, the term *seed* (*sperma*, LXX) has a plural referent. This is precisely the point that Paul *does not* make: "Now the promises were made to Abraham and to his seed. It does not say, 'And to seeds,' referring to many, but referring to one, 'And to your seed,' who is Christ" (Gal. 3:16*). For this reason some readers of the New

Testament believe that Paul is playing fast and loose with the word *seed*.[3] How are we to understand what Paul means in verse 16? The answer, I believe, is simple, but will nevertheless require a little legwork on our part.

First, we know that the word *seed* is a collective noun—in other words, it is singular in meaning but plural in its referent. I can have a handful of poppy seeds and nevertheless say that I have a handful of seed. I think the possible plurality of the word combined with the context in Genesis 15 (where God's promise of offspring emphasizes the *plurality* of Abraham's descendants), has led many to believe that *seed* always has a plural referent. But Paul points out in verse 16 that God spoke the covenantal promises to Abraham and to his *singular* seed, to one person, and this is why the Scripture does not say "and to seeds," referring to many.

Second, where does God say these things? We find the answer in two places in Genesis: "Then the LORD appeared to Abram and said, 'To your seed I will give this land.' So he built there an altar to the LORD, who had appeared to him" (Gen. 12:7*). The Abrahamic narrative also states: "And I will establish my covenant between me and you and your seed after you throughout their generations for an everlasting covenant, to be God to you and to your seed after you" (Gen. 17:7*). Even in the initial promises that God made to Abraham, he uses "seed" to refer to one person—Isaac. God made an unchanging covenantal promise that finds its fulfillment in Jesus. And he made this promise long ago, not to the New Testament church but to the patriarch of Israel—to Abraham. This is an unbroken thread that continues throughout the Old Testament.

In the very earliest portions of Scripture, God first promised Adam and Eve that the *seed* of the woman would conquer

---

3. See Richard N. Longenecker, *Biblical Exegesis in the Apostolic Period*, 2nd ed. (Grand Rapids, MI: Eerdmans, [1975] 1999), 106–107.

and crush the head of the serpent (Gen. 3:15, NKJ). When God promised to Abraham that a son would be miraculously born to Sarah, a child to be named Isaac, God reaffirmed his covenant promise to Isaac "and with his seed after him" (Gen. 17:19, KJV). God repeated this same promise to Abraham when he struggled over Sarah's instructions to cast away Ishmael and Hagar; God told Abraham, "For in Isaac your seed shall be called" (Gen. 21:12, NKJ). When God covenanted with David, he promised to give him one descendant who would build a house for God's name. This one king would reign from David's throne forever. God told David, "I will set up your seed after you . . . I will be his Father, and he shall be My son" (2 Sam. 7:12–14, NKJ). This same promise is recounted by the psalmist: "I have made a covenant with My chosen, I have sworn to My servant David: 'Your seed I will establish forever, And build up your throne to all generations'" (Psa. 89:3–4, NKJ). Now, who is the seed, the offspring of both Abraham and King David, in whom the covenant promises are fulfilled? Matthew's genealogy provides the answer: "The book of the genealogy of Jesus Christ, the son of David, the son of Abraham" (Matt. 1:1). The covenant promise to Abraham is fulfilled in Jesus Christ!

Notice what Paul says to the Galatians in the verses that follow: "This is what I mean: the law, which came 430 years afterward, does not annul a covenant previously ratified by God, so as to make the promise void" (Gal. 3:17). Paul's point is simple and yet profound. God gave the law through the Mosaic covenant four hundred thirty years *after* he made the covenant promises to Abraham. If, by giving the law, God made the promises contingent upon the obedience of his people to the law, then the covenant promise to Abraham is null and void! In his original promise, God requires nothing of Abraham—God promises to give him all of the blessings, evident by the use of the four first person personal pronouns: "And *I* will make of you a great nation, and *I* will bless you and make your name great, so that you will be a blessing. *I* will bless those who bless you, and him who dishonors you *I* will curse, and in you all the families of the earth shall be blessed" (Gen. 12:2–3; emphasis added).

Paul makes this point quite clearly: "For if the inheritance comes by the law, it no longer comes by promise; but God gave it to Abraham by a promise" (Gal. 3:18). If the inheritance—the promised covenant blessings—comes through our obedience, then it no longer comes by the covenantal promise that God made to Abraham. However, the covenant came to Abraham as a promise! Now, before we continue, there are two pressing questions. First, if the inheritance, our salvation, does not come through the law, then what purpose does the law serve? We will answer this question in the following section. Second, it seems that Paul does have in mind that the word "seed" can refer to more than one person. Note what he writes in verse 29: "And if you are Christ's, then you are Abraham's seed, and heirs according to the promise" (Gal. 3:29*). Paul is ultimately telling the Galatians that only those who are united to the one seed, to Christ, share in the blessings of the inheritance. The many who are united to Christ form one body, one church, both Jew and Gentile, united to the one seed of Abraham.

Longing and Waiting for Jesus

I hope that we see how the whole of Scripture turns upon the person of Jesus Christ. There were never two plans of salvation, one for Israel, and one for the church. Rather, the people of God have *always* looked for the coming seed; they have always looked for Jesus. Recall that faithful Simeon, a devout and righteous man, waited and longed for the consolation of Israel. Simeon did not have a hunch who the coming Messiah was; rather, the Holy Spirit opened his eyes of faith and revealed to

The Promised Seed

him that he would behold with his own eyes the long-awaited Anointed One, the promised Messiah of Yahweh. When Simeon cast his weary old eyes upon the Lord's Anointed and held him in his arms, he proclaimed: "Lord, now you are letting your servant depart in peace, according to your word; for my eyes have seen your salvation that you have prepared in the presence of all peoples, a light for revelation to the Gentiles, and for glory to your people Israel" (Luke 2:25–32). The infant King that Simeon held in his frail old arms would one day grow up and tell the disbelieving religious leaders, "Your father Abraham rejoiced that he would see my day. He saw it and was glad" (John 8:56).

Too many people believe that their salvation hinges upon their present obedience—their ability to keep the law. What they do not realize is that, in the Garden of Eden, God himself promised to save them through the mighty deeds of Christ. Thousands of years ago, God promised to bring salvation to Abraham. God's promise, not our obedience, saves us. And God fulfills that promise in his Son, Jesus Christ. This is why we must look by faith to Jesus Christ, just as Abraham did. We can rejoice, moreover, because unlike Adam, Abraham, Isaac, Jacob, or David, we no longer await the advent of Christ but live in the wonderful reality of his life, death, resurrection, and ascension.

Reflecting upon what Paul has said, I hope we discern an unshakable cause for assurance in salvation. Many of us sometimes doubt God's promises to us—we wonder whether we are really saved. Perhaps we even try to do things that will make God happy in an effort to get his blessings. We should rest—rest in the promises God has made and has brought to fulfillment in his Son. We can be assured that God promised Abraham thousands of years ago to save him and us and has been faithful to his word. For many in the church, living life is like running on a treadmill that daily increases its speed and incline. The believer tries to offer his good works in an effort to be justified, but then hears the demands for perfect obedience to the law—the treadmill picks up the pace and the incline rises—and, all the while, that person goes nowhere. He simply runs in place, growing more tired with each step as he tries to keep up the pace. The treadmill should not be an image that comes to mind when we think of the Christian life. Rather, resting in Christ should come to mind. When Christ said, "Come to me, all who labor and are heavy laden, and I will give you rest" (Matt. 11:28), he was responding to the very type of works-righteousness that too many Christians embrace.

However, when you discover that you have begun to manifest good works in your life, you should have great reason to rejoice and even gain assurance that Christ is at work in you. The apostle John, for example, writes: "Whoever keeps his word, in him truly the love of God is perfected. By this we may know that we are in him" (1 John 2:5). If you respond to hatred with love and kindness, rejoice that Christ is at work in you and that you are in him. As the Westminster Confession states, "Good works done in obedience to God's commandments, are the fruits and evidences of a true and lively faith and by them believers . . . strengthen their assurance" (16.2). Likewise, the Heidelberg Catechism explains that by good works "every one may be assured in himself of his faith, by the fruits thereof" (Q. 86). We should never rest in our good works but we can be assured by Christ, the one who ultimately stands behind them, that he holds us firmly in his grasp and will never let us go.

The natural question that arises is, "What place does the law have in the Christian's life after his conversion?" This is a question that Paul will answer in the next section. For the time being, remember that the gospel and inheritance are by faith alone in

The Promised Seed

Christ alone. If it were by the law, then it would no longer come through promise. The gospel comes through the covenantal promise of God and finds its fulfillment in Jesus Christ, the son of God, the seed of Abraham, and the seed of David.

9

Why the Law?

GALATIANS 3:19–22

Is the law then contrary to the promises of God? Certainly not! For if a law had been given that could give life, then righteousness would indeed be by the law. But the Scripture imprisoned everything under sin, so that the promise by faith in Jesus Christ might be given to those who believe.

Chances are, you have purchased something that you then had to assemble—a piece of furniture, a toy, a bicycle, or perhaps some sort of gadget for your home. How often have you opened the package, laid out the instructions, and done your best to assemble the item, but at the end, have had a few parts left over—maybe a piece of plastic, a few screws, or a large piece of wood? Your immediate thought is likely, "What have I forgotten to do?" But after you review the instructions for a long time, you come to the conclusion that maybe the part is unnecessary or perhaps was included by mistake. In other words, you are not entirely sure what to do with the leftover part. This is something like the situation that Paul addressed in his letter to the Galatian churches. He has just gone to great lengths to show how salvation and the gospel do not come through the law. So, then, why the law? Is it a leftover? Has he forgotten to include it?

Throughout the third chapter of Galatians, Paul has stressed the importance of salvation and justification by grace alone through faith alone in Christ alone. He has especially highlighted these things by pointing to God's unchanging, irrevocable covenant promise to Abraham. God made this promise to Abraham and to his seed, Jesus Christ. If the inheritance of the covenant promise were through obedience to the law, then salvation would no longer be on the basis of God's promise (Gal. 3:17–18). Paul highlights the fact that the law was given to Israel 430 years *after* God made the covenant promise to Abraham. In other words, salvation does not come through obedience to the law. If it did, then that would nullify God's covenant promise to Abraham.

Paul's claims directly counter the teachings of the Judaizers who led the Galatians to believe that their justification and salvation came through their faith in Christ *and* through circumcision, or, more broadly, their obedience to the law. Okay, simple enough—salvation comes through the promise God made to Abraham which finds its fulfillment in Christ. And the only way a person can be saved is by looking to Christ by faith. However, if this is the case, and this is how Abraham was saved, it leads to a natural question: Why the law? This is the question that Paul now sets out to answer.

Why the Law?

Paul begins this portion of chapter three with the pressing question: "Why then the law?" (Gal. 3:19a). His answer might surprise some, but notice that the law has no role for the sinner to be able to save himself through his obedience. On the contrary: "It was added because of transgressions, until the seed should come to whom the promise had been made, and it was put in place through angels by an intermediary" (Gal. 3:19*). The law was added because of transgressions, or sins.

We can get a better idea of what Paul means here by considering pertinent statements from his other writings. In his epistle to the Romans, Paul explains the function of the law: "For by works of the law no human being will be justified in his sight, since through the law comes knowledge of sin" (Rom. 3:20). Later, in the well-known fifth chapter of Romans, Paul writes: "Now the law came in to increase the trespass, but where sin increased, grace abounded all the more, so that, as sin reigned in death, grace also might reign through righteousness leading to eternal life through Jesus Christ our Lord" (Rom. 5:20–21). God wanted to accent the sinfulness of man. He wanted to make his people painfully aware of their sinful—and thus fatal—condition.

Paul expresses this idea elsewhere in Romans: "Yet if it had not been for the law, I would not have known sin. I would not have known what it is to covet if the law had not said, 'You shall not covet.' But sin, seizing an opportunity through the commandment, produced in me all kinds of covetousness. Apart from the law, sin lies dead" (Rom. 7:7–8). So then, because of man's sinfulness, God sent the law. But did God send the law merely to make Israel aware of its sinfulness without a remedy? No, not at all.

Paul writes: "It was added because of transgressions, until the offspring should come to whom the promise had been made" (Gal. 3:19). It was put in place until the seed, Jesus Christ, should come. In other words, the law had the purpose of driving Israel to the one in whom the promise of redemption would be fulfilled. Paul has more to say about this in the verses that follow. We should note another element of verse 19 that may strike us as odd at first, namely, that the law "was put in place through angels by an intermediary" (Gal. 3:19*). What does this mean, and what is its significance?

First, the law did not come directly to Israel from God: "These are the statutes and rules and laws that the LORD made between himself and the people of Israel *through* Moses on Mount Sinai" (Lev. 26:46; emphasis added). The law was revealed to Moses, and then Moses gave it to the people. Now what is not explicitly stated, though it is implied, is that Moses did not directly receive the law from God. Recall that while Moses was in God's presence, he asked to see God, but God refused and let him observe only his "back":

> Moses said, "Please show me your glory." And he said, "I will make all my goodness pass before you and will proclaim before you my name 'The LORD.' And I will be gracious to whom I will be gracious, and will show mercy on whom I will show mercy. But," he said, "you cannot see my face, for man shall not see me and live." And the LORD said, "Behold, there is a place by me where you shall stand on the rock, and while my glory passes by I will put you in a cleft of the rock, and I will cover you with my hand until I have passed by. Then I will take away my hand, and you shall see my back, but my face shall not be seen." (Exodus 33:18–23)

Implied in the fact that he could not directly behold God is that Moses did not have direct interaction with God.

Confirmation of this conclusion comes from other parts of the New Testament. In his famous sermon before the religious leaders, Stephen told the gathered crowd that Moses was "the one who was in the congregation in the wilderness with the angel who spoke to him at Mount Sinai . . . He received living oracles to give to us" (Acts 7:38). Stephen goes on to report that Israel "received the law as delivered by angels" (Acts 7:53). The author of Hebrews also writes of the angelic deliverance of the law: ". . . the message declared by angels proved to be reliable and every transgression or disobedience received a just retribution" (Heb. 2:2). God gave the law through angels to Moses, who then gave the law to Israel. So, then, what is the point here?

I think Paul's point emerges in verse 20: "Now an intermediary implies more than one, but God is one" (Gal. 3:20). This is somewhat difficult to understand at first glance. First, God made the unchanging and irrevocable covenantal promise to Abraham and his seed, Jesus Christ. God made this promise *directly* to Abraham. Moreover, this promise included both Jew and Gentile, as Abraham was to be a blessing upon all the nations of the earth. By contrast, God gave the law at Sinai *indirectly*, through mediators, through angels and through Moses, specifically to the nation of Israel, and he did this 430 years *after* he made the promise to Abraham. So, then, what does verse 20 imply?

The Abrahamic covenant, in contrast to the Mosaic covenant, more clearly sets forth God's oneness as well as his sovereignty over all creation by comprising *both* Jews and Gentiles. Paul makes this point again in Romans: "Or is God the God of Jews only? Is he not the God of Gentiles also? Yes, of Gentiles also, since God is one" (Rom. 3:29–30). So then, Paul has compared the Abrahamic and Mosaic covenants and demonstrated the superiority of the former over the latter. The Abrahamic covenant included the unchanging and irrevocable divine promise that comes directly from God through Christ and saves the people of God. The Mosaic covenant was revocable, mediated through angels and Moses, and powerless to save. Salvation comes through faith alone in Christ alone, not through obedience to the law. We have perhaps heard the saying, "Cut out the middleman and let me deal directly with the supplier." This saying aptly captures the difference between the Abrahamic and

Mosaic covenants. The Mosaic covenant had middlemen—God dealt with Moses through angels. The Abrahamic covenant had no middlemen—God dealt directly with Abraham. Similarly, we deal directly with Abraham's seed, Christ, God in the flesh, "the guarantor of a better covenant" (Heb. 7:22).

Paul continues to explain the nature of the law by answering a question likely to arise: "Is the law then contrary to the promises of God? Certainly not! For if a law had been given that could give life, then righteousness would indeed be by the law" (Gal. 3:21). Stated quite simply, given the inferiority of the covenant at Sinai to the Abrahamic covenant, does this mean that the law is contrary to or against the Abrahamic promises? Paul emphatically denies this and reemphasizes what he stated in verse 19; if God had given the law so that people could save themselves, then what need would there be for his promise to save his people? Paul counters: "But the Scripture imprisoned everything under sin, so that the promise by faith in Jesus Christ might be given to those who believe" (Gal. 3:22). God imprisoned everything under sin through the administration of the law. Note the language here—*imprisoned*. In other words, the law was never meant to give freedom but quite the opposite. "For the letter kills, but the Spirit gives life" (2 Cor. 3:6).

This is an important theme that will resurface throughout the rest of the epistle, but to give a sneak peek at what is to come, Paul characterizes the law as analogous to Pharaoh. Just as the Israelites were delivered from bondage to Pharaoh, so too Jesus delivers his people out from under the bondage of the law. Paul makes this broader point, however, at the end of verse 22: the law imprisons everything under sin to show Israel, and indeed the world, that salvation cannot come through the law. Desperate to escape the condemnation of the law and the inability to fulfill its demands, Israel and the world would turn in faith to Jesus Christ, the one who has met the demands of the

Why the Law?

law. Paul speaks to his audience in terms they will understand, painting a grand picture with the ideas, images, and words connected to the Old Testament Exodus.

The Law and Sanctification

It is vastly important, not only for our salvation but also for our sanctification, that we understand what Paul has explained here in verses 19–22. Immediately, as it concerns Paul's point, his explanation of the law clearly refutes the teaching of the Judaizers. Our salvation is not a combination of our faith in Christ plus our good works. Salvation and justification come through God's grace alone through faith alone in Christ alone.

As we look into the face of the law, it reveals our sin; it shows us the myriad ways in which we fall short of its demands. And then upon seeing our sinfulness, just as in our conversion, we look to Christ for our sanctification. We are made holier by fleeing to Christ who by the indwelling power of the Holy Spirit produces his fruit within us. As John Murray explains:

> It is imperative that we realize our complete dependence upon the Holy Spirit. We must not forget, of course, that our activity is enlisted to the fullest extent in the process of sanctification. But we must not rely upon our own strength of resolution or purpose. It is when we are weak that we are strong. It is by grace that we are being saved as surely as by grace we have been saved.[1]

In other words, as we work out our salvation in our quest for holiness, are we relying upon ourselves and our own strength or the grace of God in Christ?

Our union with Christ by the indwelling power and presence of the Holy Spirit produces our obedience. Suffice it to

---

1. John Murray, *Redemption Accomplished and Applied* (Grand Rapids, MI: Eerdmans, 1955), 147.

say that if we try to pursue holiness and sanctification solely through obedience to the law, we, like Israel, are trying to return to the very bondage from which we have been freed:

> For the law of the Spirit of life has set you free in Christ Jesus from the law of sin and death. For God has done what the law, weakened by the flesh, could not do. By sending his own Son in the likeness of sinful flesh and for sin, he condemned sin in the flesh, in order that the righteous requirement of the law might be fulfilled in us, who walk not according to the flesh but according to the Spirit. (Rom. 8:2–4)

Though we must pursue our sanctification through Christ and not the law, this does not mean that there is no place for the law of God in the Christian life. Paul certainly talks about the importance of the law for the Christian, something that he will address in subsequent chapters; namely, the key idea that faith must "work through love" (Gal. 5:6) and that loving your neighbor is to fulfill the law (Gal. 5:14). Having emphasized the second use of the law (to expose our sin), we cannot ignore the third (or normative) use of the law. In the third use of the law, justified believers look to it in order to know what conduct pleases our heavenly father. The Westminster Confession thus states that the law is "a rule of life informing them [believers] of the will of God, and of their duty, it directs and binds them to walk accordingly" (19.6). The law, therefore, is immensely important for our sanctification, but believers must use it properly and never apart from Christ. The law in its normative (or third) use is not the actual road upon which we travel, but the guardrails on either side of the road. The road on which we travel is Christ. Like guardrails, the law shows us where the path of righteousness lies and keeps us traveling on it. Or in biblical terms, the ladder to heaven is always Christ, never the law (cf. Gen 28:12; John 1:51).

Why the Law?

So, then, let us briefly summarize what Paul has established. It is of the utmost importance that we understand him, not only for our justification but also for our sanctification. Our salvation is based in the Abrahamic covenant, not the Mosaic covenant. The Abrahamic covenant finds its fulfillment in Christ, the one who both fulfills the requirement of obedience and also bears the curse of the law on behalf of those who look to him in faith. The law is powerless to give life; it came 430 years after the covenant promise to Abraham, and was given indirectly by God through angels and Moses. The law, nevertheless, is not contrary to the gospel promise but instead drives us to Christ, the one who has fulfilled the obligations of the law. Law and gospel work in concert to bring about the salvation of God's people. But we must carefully delineate the different functions of law and gospel—the law threatens and condemns, but the gospel saves. If these things are true, then we have no other option but to look into the mirror of the law, see our sin, and then flee to Christ in faith, both in our justification and sanctification, our conversion and our Christian life. Therefore, flee to Christ that he may save you from the curse of the law and cause you to walk in God's statutes through the indwelling and sanctifying power of the Holy Spirit.

10

Sons of Abraham, Sons of God

GALATIANS 3:23–29

But now that faith has come, we are no longer under a guardian, for in Christ Jesus you are all sons of God, through faith. For as many of you as were baptized into Christ have put on Christ. There is neither Jew nor Greek, there is neither slave nor free, there is no male and female, for you are all one in Christ Jesus. And if you are Christ's, then you are Abraham's offspring, heirs according to promise.

In the ancient world, the first-born son had a number of privileges that his siblings did not share. He was entitled to a double portion of his family's inheritance. In addition to this financial blessing, the first-born son was also considered the head of the family and the leader among his siblings. If there were any female offspring, they usually did not receive an inheritance, as only male heirs could inherit the family wealth. In many ways, Paul takes these traditions and turns them upside down:

because Christ is the first-born over all creation (Col. 1:16), all of those united to him become heirs to tremendous blessings. First, however, let us review what Paul has covered thus far.

Paul has shown the Galatians three main things. First, God made an inviolable, unchanging covenantal promise directly to Abraham, one ultimately fulfilled in Abraham's seed, Jesus Christ. Second, this promise, as we will especially see in the text before us, embraces both the Jews and the Gentiles, because God promised Abraham that through him all the families of the earth would be blessed. In other words, the gospel was not simply a blessing upon Abraham and the Jews but upon the Gentiles as well. Third, the covenant that God made through Moses was 430 years after the promises to Abraham; it was temporary, and it was made indirectly to Israel through the mediation of angels and Moses. Paul's chief point in contrasting the two covenants is to show that if salvation came through obedience to the law, then it would nullify and void the promise that God made to Abraham. However, the law was never intended to give life. Rather, it was added because of transgressions—it was added to reveal sin, thereby increasing the awareness of guiltiness. This way, salvation was and always has been through the promise. The two covenants, however, were not opposed to one another but rather worked in tandem. The Mosaic covenant was intended to drive Israel to Christ, the one in whom the covenant promise to Abraham is fulfilled.

Now, in the passage before us, Paul continues to explain the nature and role of the law and the Mosaic covenant. By showing the nature of the law, he makes an emphatic point about the nature of the people of God. Namely, through the promise, there is neither Jew nor Gentile, slave nor free, male nor female. Rather, he makes the stunning point that all who are in Christ are sons both of Abraham and of God.

Sons of Abraham, Sons of God

Imprisoned Under the Law

Paul writes: "Now before faith came, we were held captive under the law, imprisoned until the coming faith would be revealed" (Gal. 3:23). Once again, Paul uses the language of slavery to characterize our former relationship to the law. The Judaizers thought that circumcision would bring them freedom from Satan, sin, and death, but Paul points out that it brings the exact opposite. He says that until "faith came," which is defined in the next verse as the advent of Jesus Christ, everything was "held captive" and "imprisoned" under the law: "But the Scripture imprisoned everything under sin, so that the promise by faith in Jesus Christ might be given to those who believe" (Gal. 3:22).[1] So then, the law kept people in bondage. It accused Israel of its sinfulness, showing them their inability to keep the law. Did God do this with no remedy in view? Absolutely not.

Paul writes in verse 24: "So then, the law was our guardian until Christ came, in order that we might be justified by faith." Paul uses some interesting language to describe the law. He says that the law, the Mosaic covenant, was "our guardian" until Christ came. What does he mean by this? Paul uses the Greek term *paidagogos*, which should sound familiar to us, as it is the word from which we get the word *pedagogue*. The King James translates the word *schoolmaster*.

In Paul's day, this word referred to a hired person or slave who was supposed to train the children of the family. The schoolmaster or guardian was supposed to train the children in basic knowledge, writing, and arithmetic, but also in issues of morals.[2] We might say that the schoolmaster or guardian was something like a nanny. The schoolmaster or guardian was also supposed to punish the children if they misbehaved as well

---

1. Thomas Schreiner, *Galatians*, ZECNT (Grand Rapids, MI: Zondervan, 2010), 245.

2. Schreiner, *Galatians*, 248.

as protect them from the influence of outsiders. These ideas (teaching, punishing, and setting apart) inform Paul's use of this term for the Mosaic covenant.

The schoolmaster was supposed to teach Israel about the coming Messiah through its ceremonies, sacrifices, and laws—these things pointed forward to the perfect sacrifice and righteousness of the coming Messiah. The schoolmaster was supposed to punish the Israelites by revealing to them their sin and prescribing sanctions for those sins. The schoolmaster was supposed to set Israel apart from the nations by protecting her from the paganism and idolatry that had polluted the previous inhabitants of the Promised Land. But notice that the schoolmaster had a temporary function: "So then, the law was our guardian *until Christ came*, in order that we might be justified by faith" (Gal. 3:24; emphasis added). The schoolmaster was supposed to operate until Christ came. And to what end? That the people of God might be justified by faith.

In other words, justification, the divine declaration that we are counted as righteous, does not come through the law—not through the guardian—but through faith in Christ: "But now that faith has come, we are no longer under a guardian" (Gal. 3:25). We are no longer under the tutelage of the schoolmaster now that Christ has been revealed. Those who look to Christ by faith alone have been freed from the imprisonment of the schoolmaster: "For in Christ Jesus you are all sons of God, through faith" (Gal. 3:26). This is the first lightning bolt that Paul delivers: namely, that if a person believes in Jesus Christ, then he is a son of God.

Son of God is a staggering designation. The Jews historically thought of themselves as having a privileged status because God chose them out of all the nations of the earth. In this sense, we know that God looked upon the nation of Israel as his very own son (Exod. 4:22). God lamented over Israel in strongly paternal terms: "When Israel was a child, I loved him, and out of Egypt I called my son" (Hos. 11:1). Paul says that *anyone*, Jew or Gentile, who looks to Christ by faith is a son of God! Paul drives this point home even further: "For as many of you as were baptized into Christ have put on Christ. There is neither Jew nor Greek, there is neither slave nor free, there is neither male nor female, for you are all one in Christ Jesus. And if you are Christ's, then you are Abraham's seed, heirs according to promise" (Gal. 3:27–29*).

Believers in Christ are therefore baptized into his name; they have put him on. Paul makes the stunning claim that, in Christ, there is neither Jew nor Greek. There are no racial privileges in Christ. A Gentile need not become a Jew to inherit the blessings of the covenant promise to Abraham. In Christ, there is neither slave nor free. Whether a person is the wealthiest of the wealthy or on the lowest rung of the social ladder (e.g., a slave in Paul's day), such distinctions are levelled in Christ. Wealth does nothing to improve one's standing in the sight of God. Moreover, there is neither male nor female in Christ. In Paul's day women were accorded a lower social standing than men. In fact, a single, solitary woman was not a person in the eyes of the law—she could not bring legal testimony in a court of law by herself. Rather, two women were required to bring testimony in a court of law, whereas a solitary man could testify in a court of law by himself. Additionally, a woman in Paul's day could not own property in Israel. But, in Christ, no such social standings exist. Rather, a woman who is baptized into Christ was treated, not as a daughter, but as a *son* of God. It was the sons of a man who received the family inheritance, and, even more specifically, it was the firstborn son who received a double portion of the inheritance. Daughters had no standing in terms of the inheritance (cf. Num. 27:1–11).

Nevertheless, those women who are in Christ are treated as *sons* and they too receive the promised inheritance, the blessings of the covenant that God made to Abraham. And for this reason, Paul concludes by saying that not only is a person who looks to Christ by faith a son of God, but he or she is also Abraham's seed. Once again, such a conclusion is dramatic, as it completely collides with the teaching of the Judaizers who believed that a Gentile had to be circumcised in order to be saved. Paul demonstrates from the Scriptures, however, that what the Judaizers were trying to give the Gentiles through the law—by returning to the schoolmaster and its bondage—God already gave through faith from the very beginning.

What Makes Us Pleasing To God?

To say that Paul's message is still relevant is an understatement. As with the previous chapter, we regularly need to hear about the nature of the law and what purpose it serves. We are all good legalists at heart, and, from time to time, we think that our obedience somehow impresses God and causes him to look upon us with greater favor. We do this every time we look down on someone who does not live exactly like we do. We always find some way to compare ourselves favorably with our neighbors so we can think ourselves better than they: whether it be in the clothes we wear, cars we drive, books we read, music we listen to, food we eat, the way we recreate, the way we educate our children, or whatever the case might be. We find something to latch on to, and then we measure others in the church by our own standard rather than God's. The Judaizers latched on to circumcision and demanded that the Gentiles toe the line so that they could be saved. If we recognize that our various activities do not make us holy, but we are holy in Christ, then we will be able to appreciate and better understand what Paul has said. We cannot offer anything of ourselves to improve our standing before the Lord. Rather, our union with Christ by faith makes us pleasing to God. Our union with him makes us sons of God and sons of Abraham.

Sons of Abraham, Sons of God

We should also note how so many within the church rob themselves of this hope by trying to "improve" the message of Scripture. A number of translations (the New Revised Standard Version, the New Living Translation, the New American Bible, and Today's New International Version) attempt to eliminate the impression that Paul excludes women in verse 26 by replacing "sons" with the more gender-neutral "children". For example, the NRSV states: "For in Christ Jesus you are all ~~sons~~ [children] of God through faith."

Replacing the word "sons" with "children" essentially negates Paul's point. Yes, of course, we are God's children through faith in Christ. But, more specifically, we are all, male and female, God's *sons*. To call a woman a "son" does not negate her femininity but rather accords her the same covenantal legal status as a full heir in Christ! In other words, we all, male *and* female, receive the promised inheritance in Christ—both receive equal status, both filial and legal standing in the covenant. While fiddling with the translation might give us a sense of security that the Bible has not excluded women from its promises, we should wonder whether the supposed rewards of feminism and political correctness are worth obscuring the inheritance that we all have in Christ. Too often, we are so interested in telling God what he should do or what we have done that we fail to hear what *he* has done for us in Christ.

I hope we have seen and understood what Paul has written. I hope we understand the function of the law relative to justification—that it drives us to Christ by revealing our sin and shows us Christ in the foreshadows of the law, the sacrifices, and ceremonies. I also hope we see that the covenant promises that God made to Abraham come, not through anything that we ourselves can bring and give to God, but only through what he condescends to give us, namely, faith in Christ. Moreover, our redemption comes through our union with Christ by faith alone. We become sons of the living God and sons of Abraham. The promised inheritance comes to us through faith in Christ. Cling and hold fast, therefore, to the promises that God made to Abraham, fulfilled in Christ, and know that whether Jew or Greek, slave or free, male or female, we are all one in Christ Jesus.

11

No Longer Slaves

GALATIANS 4:1–7

But when the fullness of time had come, God sent forth his Son, born of woman, born under the law, to redeem those who were under the law, so that we might receive adoption as sons. And because you are sons, God has sent the Spirit of his Son into our hearts, crying, "Abba! Father!" So you are no longer a slave, but a son, and if a son, then an heir through God.

Just the word, *adoption*, can conjure a cloud of negative associations for many people, since adoptions are frequently necessitated by abandonment, poverty, illness, and the like. After all, why else would a child be an orphan except that his parents did not want him or could not provide for him? Or perhaps the child had a crippling illness and the prospects of caring for him seemed too daunting. In any case, these negative circumstances are certainly linked to adoption in our minds, but there is also a flip side to the coin. For every unwanted child who is adopted, there is a set of adoptive parents who specifically chose him. They chose him regardless of the cost or challenges involved.

They gave him their family name and granted him full rights as a member of their family. This is the theme of the passage before us, namely, how God adopts a sinful and rebellious people and grants them the rights and privileges of sons.

Paul has already made the striking claim that *anyone*—no matter their social status, ethnicity, or gender—who is in Christ, who looks to Christ by faith, is a son of God and a son of Abraham. In the passage before us, Paul continues to expand these same themes, though he does so from a slightly different perspective. Paul centers our attention on the work of Christ and one of the many benefits that it brings—namely, our *adoption* as God's sons.

Enslaved to the Elementary Principles

Paul begins by contrasting life as an heir with life as a slave: "I mean that the heir, as long as he is a child, is no different from a slave, though he is the owner of everything, but he is under guardians and managers until the date set by his father" (Gal. 4:1–2). Paul, building on imagery he employed towards the end of chapter 3, continues to develop the idea of the schoolmaster. The apostle explains that as long as an heir is a child he is no different than a slave. Even though a young child might be the heir to an empire, he must remain under the guardianship of a schoolmaster due to his young age or immaturity until the child's father decides that the time has come for his son to become independent. The child, in other words, is not free.

Paul now connects this analogy to Israel's existence under the law: "In the same way we also, when we were children, were enslaved to the elementary principles of the world" (Gal. 4:3). Here Paul says that during its early existence, Israel was enslaved to the elementary principles of the world. What does this phrase mean, the "elementary principles of the world" (*stoicheia*)? In a Greek philosophical context, the term *stoicheia* referred to the primary elements: earth, water, fire, and air. Paul uses *stoicheia* according to this sense in his epistle to the Colossians: "See to it that no one takes you captive by philosophy and empty deceit, according to human tradition, according to the elemental spirits of the world [*stoicheia*], and not according to Christ" (Col. 2:8). In other scriptural contexts, *stoicheia* refers to the basic teachings of Scripture: "For though by this time you ought to be teachers, you need someone to teach you again the basic principles [*stoicheia*] of the oracles of God. You need milk, not solid food" (Heb. 5:12). What then does Paul mean by this term in Galatians?

In context, the primary referent is the Mosaic covenant. Note the parallel language Paul employs to describe life under the Mosaic covenant: "Now before faith came, we were held captive under the law, imprisoned until the coming faith would be revealed. So then, the law was our guardian until Christ came, in order that we might be justified by faith" (Gal. 3:23–24). However, the primary significance is the idea that Israel was imprisoned under the law, under the Mosaic covenant. Secondarily, for Gentiles not under the Mosaic covenant but later turned to Christ in faith, Paul's use of the term *stoicheia* would be a reminder that they were once imprisoned under the vain teachings of man, but now in Christ, were set free (cf. Gal. 4:8). Paul characterizes life under the schoolmaster, or the *stoicheia*, as a life of slavery, whether under paganism or under the Mosaic covenant: "But the Scripture imprisoned everything under sin, so that the promise by faith in Jesus Christ might be given to those who believe" (Gal. 3:22). Israel was under the curse of the law and imprisoned to it because of their sin as well as because of their inability to fulfill its demands.

But as Paul constantly reminds his readers, God did not leave Israel in despair and without hope: "But when the fullness of time had come, God sent forth his Son, born of woman, born under the law, to redeem those who were under the law, so that we might receive adoption as sons" (Gal. 4:4–5). God sent his Son, Jesus, in the fullness of time. From the beginning of redemptive history, God's people have awaited the advent of Christ. We can trace the hope of God's people all the way back to the jubilant declaration of Eve that she had given birth to the Messiah, the Lord incarnate (Gen. 4:1).[1] Eve eventually had her hopes dashed as Cain proved to be no Messiah but rather a murderer (Gen. 4:8). God's people nevertheless continued to anticipate the advent of the Christ, the seed of Shem (Gen. 9), Abraham, Isaac, Jacob, David, and many others (Matt. 1:1ff).

They looked with longing to the hope of the last days when the Lion of the Tribe of Judah would come (Gen. 49:1, 8–10).[2] The faithful people of God continued to hope for a prophet who would come, one like Moses (Deut. 18:15). At the height of Israel's stature among the nations and the glory of the monarchy, faithful Israel sought shelter in the promises of a Davidic descendant (2 Sam. 7:14). Yet even in the depths and darkness of exile in Babylon, the people of God longed for the time when God himself would come to inaugurate a covenant; not like the one that he made with Israel when they came out of Egypt, which they promptly broke, falling under its curse, but a new covenant (Jer. 31:31–32). When all of these things had come to pass, when redemptive history was pregnant and ready to give birth to the Messiah, John the Baptist announced to the crowds that gathered around him: "The time is fulfilled, and the kingdom of God is at hand; repent and believe in the gospel" (Mark 1:15). With the advent of Christ, the fulfillment of the Messianic expectation has come.

---

1. See Martin Luther, *Lectures on Genesis: Chapters 1–5*, vol. 1, *Luther's Works*, ed. Jaroslav Pelikan (St. Louis: Concordia Publishing House, 1958), 241–243.

2. Geerhardus Vos, *The Eschatology of the Old Testament*, ed. James T. Dennison, Jr. (Phillipsburg, NJ: P&R, 2001), 89–104.

No Longer Slaves

In the fullness of time, God sent forth his son, born of a woman; and note especially that he was born *under the law*. In other words, Jesus came to fulfill the requirements of the law on behalf of those who could not do it, even from his infancy! Luke recounts that Jesus was dedicated to the Lord in his infancy "according to the Law of Moses" (Luke 2:22–24). Paul revisits a theme he raised earlier in his epistle: "Christ redeemed us from the curse of the law by becoming a curse for us" (Gal. 3:13a). The obedience of Christ results in the adoption as sons for those who look to Christ by faith.

Paul now elaborates on the nature of our adoption: "And because you are sons, God has sent the Spirit of his Son into our hearts, crying, 'Abba! Father!' So you are no longer a slave, but a son, and if a son, then an heir through God" (Gal. 4:6–7). By the Father's grace through the work of Christ, which is received by faith alone, God has sent his Holy Spirit into our hearts to bring about our adoption. And if we are adopted as God's sons, then we no longer know God as judge but only as our heavenly Father. And if we know God as Father, then we can cry out to him for our every need. That Paul says we can cry "Abba! Father!" is also unique, as it is a term of intimacy. Paul contrasts the freedom and divine sonship that we have by faith through Christ with the bondage and alienation we had in our attempts to secure redemption through our own obedience. He explains that the Galatians are no longer slaves, that is, imprisoned under the law, but rather they are God's sons. And if they are God's sons, then they are therefore heirs of the covenant promises that God made to Abraham, whether Jew or Gentile, slave or free, male or female.

An orphan owns nothing and has rights to very little, if anything. But when an orphan is adopted by loving parents, legally he now has a family, a new last name, and an inheritance. The orphan is no longer an orphan. Everything that is true of the adopted orphan is even more true of the person who is saved and adopted by God. The Westminster Confession offers a wonderful summary of all of the blessings of our adoption in Christ:

> All those that are justified, God vouchsafes, in and for his only Son Jesus Christ, to make partakers of the grace of adoption, by which they are taken into the number, and enjoy the liberties and privileges of the children of God, have his name put upon them, receive the Spirit of adoption, have access to the throne of grace with boldness, are enabled to cry, Abba, Father, are pitied, protected, provided for, and chastened by him, as by a father: yet never cast off, but sealed to the day of redemption; and inherit the promises, as heirs of everlasting salvation. (12.1)

In summary, our adoption in Christ affords us a great number of blessings we did not know before but will never lose.

The Old Testament Foreshadows Salvation in Christ

We should unpack the Old Testament events to which Paul has implicitly made reference. First, Paul has used the language of imprisonment, captivity, and slavery to describe Israel's relationship to the law. This language points us to Israel's past, particularly Israel's bondage in Egypt.[3] The bottom line is that the Old Testament Exodus foreshadowed the redemption that would come through Christ. Israel was in bondage and had Pharaoh as a cruel taskmaster who burdened Israel with an unbearable workload. God, however, delivered Israel by his mighty hand. Israel was God's son (Exod. 4:22), but was nevertheless imprisoned under a cruel overlord. Pharaoh released God's son, but then pursued him to the Red Sea, where God miraculously

---

3. James M. Scott, *Adoption as Sons of God* (Tübingen, Germany: Mohr Siebeck, 1992), 121–186.

delivered him. During that time Israel was led during the day by a cloud, and at night by a pillar of fire. What was the significance of the cloud? Or, more specifically, *who* is the cloud? The Scriptures elsewhere tell us that the Holy Spirit was present during the Red Sea crossing (Isa. 63:11; Hag. 2:4–5). These Old Testament passages indicate that the cloud was the Holy Spirit.

So then, notice the overall pattern here—Israel, God's son, was delivered from Pharaoh's bondage and then God placed his Holy Spirit in their midst by bringing them through the Red Sea, an event described by Paul elsewhere as a *baptism* (1 Cor. 10:1–4). Consider Paul's statements again against this backdrop:

> In the same way we also, when we were children, were enslaved to the elementary principles of the world. But when the fullness of time had come, God sent forth his Son, born of woman, born under the law, to redeem those who were under the law, so that we might receive adoption as sons. And because you are sons, God has sent the Spirit of his Son into our hearts, crying, "Abba! Father!" (Galatians 4:3–6)

Paul employs Israel's history, their slavery in Egypt, to characterize their bondage to the law. Israel was incapable of freeing themselves. But what Israel was unable to do, God did through Christ. For the Judaizers to seek salvation and justification through obedience to the law was like Israel wanting to forfeit their freedom, surrender their relationship with God as their father, and return to bondage and slavery under Pharaoh. This is why Paul was so exercised—the Judaizers were trying to turn back the clock and live as though Christ had never come. Indeed, they were trying to accomplish what only Christ could accomplish, what only he *did* accomplish. So, then, we must continue to look to Christ for what only he can do. We must not seek to return to the bondage and slavery of the law, for to do so means death.

We must therefore seek life in Christ by trusting in what he has done on our behalf: receiving the perfect righteousness achieved by his obedience to the law, suffering the curse of the law in his crucifixion, defeating the powers of sin and death in his resurrection, and ascending to the right hand of the Father in royal session. At the same time, we should not forget what Christ's work brings us, namely our adoption as God's sons. We are God's sons. Do we therefore cry out to him, "Abba, Father!"? If our heavenly Father has redeemed us from the clutches of Satan, sin, and death by giving us his only begotten Son, then why would he withhold from us the things we need and even desire? As Paul elsewhere writes: "What then shall we say to these things? If God is for us, who can be against us? He who did not spare his own Son but gave him up for us all, how will he not also with him graciously give us all things?" (Rom. 8:31–32).

How often do we seek things from so many other places, people, and institutions, but never bring our needs to our heavenly Father in prayer? Do we seek contentment in material things? Do we seek personal worth, value, and self-esteem from our friends and family? Do we seek financial security in our investments, our jobs, and savings accounts? Do we have strong desires in our lives, dreams to see our children grow up and be godly, to have strong marriages, to lead godly lives? So often we pursue these things vainly in our own strength forgetting the one person who can give them to us. Our heavenly Father is not stingy—he will see to our every need. Our heavenly Father is not cruel: he will fulfill the desires of our hearts as they conform to his will.

Seek our heavenly Father in all things; seek his face in prayer. Cry out to him, "Abba, Father!" and pray that he would, by the power of his Holy Spirit, conform you to the image of his Son and fulfill your every need and desire. Do not seek to do for yourself what only God can do through his Son and by his Holy

Spirit. But at the same time, if we are adopted as God's sons and are now heirs to the riches of his grace in Christ, then we should always remember our identity, whose name we bear. As Peter writes: "As obedient children, do not be conformed to the passions of your former ignorance, but as he who called you is holy, you also be holy in all your conduct" (1 Pet. 1:14–15). God has not adopted us so that we would continue under the bondage and slavery to Satan, sin, death, and the condemnation of the law. Rather, empowered by the grace of God in our union with Christ, we should always seek to manifest the righteousness and holiness to which God calls us.

12

Never Go Back

GALATIANS 4:8–11

---

*Formerly, when you did not know God, you were enslaved
to those that by nature are not gods. But now that you
have come to know God, or rather to be known by God,
how can you turn back again to the weak and worthless elementary principles of the world, whose slaves you
want to be once more? You observe days and months and
seasons and years! I am afraid I may have labored over
you in vain.*

I once watched a documentary that recounted the torturous
existence of downed American pilots living in the infamous
"Hanoi Hilton" during the Vietnam War. A number of these airmen spent years as prisoners of war enduring excruciating conditions—starvation, torture, and barbarous living quarters. A
peace was finally negotiated and these airmen were returned to
the United States. The documentary recounted how the former
prisoners were given medical attention, bathed, and given new
clothes. When they first arrived at their initial destination in
the Philippines, they were brought into the on-base cafeteria

and told that they could eat whatever and however much they wanted—the cooks would make anything for them. One airman ordered a large steak, a dozen eggs, and French toast. To say the least, these former prisoners were elated to be freed from captivity. What if, however, you discovered that these former prisoners wanted to back to the Hanoi Hilton? What if they told their superiors that they wanted to return to captivity? Would not people think they were insane?

This illustration reflects something of Paul's frustration with the Galatians. The apostle explains in this passage that they had been freed from slavery to the law, so why would they want to go back? Why would they want to go back under the curse of the law if Christ had freed them from it? Paul's point is this: Only the perfect law-keeping of Christ can deliver from the curse of the law. Only God in Christ could extract man from his sinful estate and meet the law's demand of absolute perfection. In spite of the God-given, Christ-wrought, Spirit-applied freedom from Satan, sin, and death, redeemed man still tries to return to the very slavery and bondage from which he has just been delivered. Before we proceed, though, we should note that Paul continues to use the narrative backdrop of Israel's Exodus in his refutation of the false teachers.

Delivered from Pagan gods

In the opening of this section, Paul writes: "Formerly, when you did not know God, you were enslaved to those that by nature are not gods" (Gal. 4:8). He turns his attention to the Gentiles in the Galatian churches and reminds them of their former slavery. Recall what Paul has written just a few verses prior: "In the same way we also, when we were children, were enslaved to the elementary principles of the world" (Gal. 4:3; cf. Col. 2:8; Heb. 5:12). So, then, it seems that Paul has the Gentiles in view and reminds them of their former slavery to vain human philosophy and the worship of false gods, which Paul explains are not truly gods. Paul asks them how they could desire to forfeit their freedom: "But now that you have come to know God, or rather to be known by God, how can you turn back again to the weak and worthless elementary principles of the world, whose slaves you want to be once more?" (Gal. 4:9). Paul contrasts their ignorance of God in their pre-Christian lives with their knowledge of God in Christ.

Notice, however, the subtle shift in the voice of Paul's verbs. Paul writes: "Now that you have come to know God"—the infinitive "to know" (*gnontes*) is in the active voice. But Paul then quickly qualifies what he means: "or rather to be known by God"—here the verb *gnosthentes* changes to the passive voice. Why the difference? In the former, the human being seeks God and finds him. In the latter, God seeks the sinful person, finds, and saves him. In the former, human initiative brings salvation. In the latter, the sovereign initiative of God brings salvation. Despite his greatest efforts to scale the heavens, a la the tower of Babel, man is incapable of reaching God. The only way that man can be saved is if God descends from the heights and reaches down to save man from himself. As Dorothy Sayers once wrote:

> Now, we may call that doctrine exhilarating or we may call it devastating; we may call it Revelation or we may call it rubbish; but if we call it dull, then words have no meaning at all. That God should play the tyrant over man is a dismal story of unrelieved oppression; that man should play the tyrant over man is the usual dreary record of human futility; but that man should play the tyrant over God and find Him a better man than himself is an astonishing drama indeed. Any journalist, hearing of it for the first time, would recognize it as News; those who did hear it for the first time actually called it News, and good news at that; though we are apt to

> forget that the word *Gospel* ever meant anything so sensational.[1]

Such is the dramatic nature of the gospel, and why Paul was so concerned for the Galatians. Only *God* saves us from sin and the curse of the law.

Ironically, the Gentiles in the Galatian churches were using their God-given freedom to turn back to the very slavery from which they had been freed: "But now that you have come to know God, or rather to be known by God, how can you turn back again to the weak and worthless elementary principles of the world, whose slaves you want to be once more?" (Gal. 4:9). Just like Israel wanting to return to the pots of meat in Egypt, so too the Gentile and Jewish Christians were wanting to return to the bondage of the elementary principles of the world. For the Gentiles, taking circumcision upon them as a means of salvation and justification was like returning to the bondage of the vain philosophies and false deities they once worshipped. Likewise, for the Jews, to take circumcision upon them as a means of salvation and justification, was to return to the imprisonment of the law, the elementary teachings of the Scriptures. For both Jew and Gentile it was an attempt to turn back the clock and live as if Christ had never come.

In the following verse, an almost flabbergasted Paul criticizes the Galatians for observing even "days and months and seasons and years!" (Gal. 4:10). The days likely in view are the celebration of the Sabbath and the various feast days of the Old Testament: the Day of Atonement, the Feast of Booths, Passover, the Feast of Weeks, and the Feast of Trumpets (Lev. 23). Paul in no way intended to imply that the moral demands of the law had been abrogated or canceled. Wherever the moral law is found—whether written upon the heart of man, given to Adam

---

1. Dorothy L. Sayers, *Creed—or—Chaos? Why Christians Must Choose Either Dogma or Disaster (Or, Why it Really Does Matter What You Believe)* (Manchester, NH: Sophia Institute Press, [1949] 1974), 12.

and Eve in the Garden of Eden, or summarized in the Ten Commandments at Mt. Sinai—it is universally binding upon all people (cf. Gen. 1:26–28; 2:16–17; Exod. 20:1–17; Lev. 18:5; Deut. 5:1–21; Rom. 2:14–15; 10:5; Gal. 3:10–12; WCF 19.1–2, 5). But Paul's point exposes one of the most fundamental exegetical problems the church has had, namely, the relationship between the Old and New Testaments, and what have been called the *ceremonial* and *civil* aspects of the law. And, therefore, I think this point deserves more attention.

Christians often appeal to the Old Testament as if Christ had never come. This happens, for example, when people appeal to the Ten Commandments as if they were things that we need to do in order to be saved, which is a misunderstanding of how the moral law functions (cf. WCF 19.5–6). They appeal to the Israelite particulars of the Old Testament civil law as if they compose the standard by which we are supposed to regulate the United States government today (cf. WCF 19.4). Seventh-day Adventists, for example, continue to hold corporate worship on the last day of the week, Saturday, the old Sabbath, which is a misunderstanding of the ceremonial law (cf. WCF 19.3). Or, at least in Paul's case, the Jewish Christians were still celebrating many of the feast days of the Old Testament. The fundamental error involved in such practices, whether in Paul's day or our own, is the failure to grasp the concept that the Old Testament prefigures the person and work of Christ in its key persons, institutions, ceremonies, and rites. St. Augustine (354–430) once explained, the old is revealed in the new, and the new is hidden in the old. We may look at the Old Testament as the promise and the New Testament as the fulfillment. Still yet, and more technically, we should understand that the Old Testament is the shadow, or type, and the New Testament is the *reality* to which the shadows point, or the *antitype*.[2]

---

2. See Leonhard Goppelt, *Typos: The Typological Interpretation of the Old Testament in the New* (Grand Rapids, MI: Eerdmans, 1982).

Consider a few passages of Scripture to substantiate this relationship between the Old Testament and New Testament: "Yet death reigned from Adam to Moses, even over those whose sinning was not like the transgression of Adam, who was a *type* of the one who was to come" (Rom. 5:14; emphasis added). Paul explains that Adam is a type of the one to come, namely Jesus—Adam is a "rough sketch," if you will, of Christ. Notice the relationship between the two Adams that Paul establishes elsewhere:

> Thus it is written, "The first man Adam became a living being"; the last Adam became a life-giving Spirit . . . As was the man of dust, so also are those who are of the dust, and as is the man of heaven, so also are those who are of heaven. Just as we have borne the image of the man of dust, we shall also bear the image of the man of heaven. (1 Corinthians 15:45, 48–49*; cf. Genesis 2:7)

Adam prefigures the last Adam, Jesus. But Adam is not the only one who foreshadows Christ.

Moses as the shepherd of Israel looks forward to Christ the true Shepherd (Heb. 3:3–6). Aaron as the high priest looks forward to Christ, the true High Priest (Heb. 7–8). David as the king of Israel looks forward to Christ, the King of kings (2 Sam. 7:14; Psa. 110:1). The prophets all anticipate and look forward to Christ, the ultimate Prophet (Deut. 18:15–22). The institutions and ceremonies of the Old Testament point forward to the person and work of Christ. The author of Hebrews, for example, explains that the first tabernacle foreshadowed the person and work of Christ. As long as the veil separated the outer tabernacle from the holy of holies, it meant that the Messiah had not come and the last days, the in-breaking of the new heavens and earth, had not yet dawned (Heb. 9:8–9). But when Christ came, the sacrifices, rites, and ceremonies that pointed to Christ to come were abolished. God abolished the old order to establish the new one (Heb. 10:9). Paul succinctly states this same truth elsewhere: "Therefore let no one pass judgment on you in questions of food and drink, or with regard to a festival or a new moon or a Sabbath. These are a shadow of the things to come, but the substance belongs to Christ" (Col. 2:16–17).

The Judaizers failed to grasp the proper relationship between the Old and New Testaments. This is especially so concerning circumcision. The Old Testament rite pointed forward to the crucifixion, the circumcison, or *cutting off*, of Christ from the benevolent presence of God. This circumcision brought the outpouring of the Holy Spirit and his effectual calling of the elect, the circumcision of the heart, one made without hands (Col. 2:11). For these reasons Paul lets out a sigh of discouragement and writes: "I am afraid I may have labored over you in vain" (Gal. 4:11). He feared all was lost because they were trying to turn back the clock—they were returning to the bondage of the law rather than living in the Christ-given freedom from the curse of the law. They were regressing from the light to the darkness, from grace to law, from the freedom of the wilderness to the bondage of Egypt.

Our Inability to Save Ourselves

There are several things that should strike us here; chief among them is the idea that we cannot save ourselves. We must therefore come to grips with our depravity, our sinfulness. We must give assent to the biblical doctrine that we are utterly sinful and unable to save ourselves. As Paul says, no one is righteous, no, not one (Rom. 3:10). All have fallen short of the glory of God (Rom. 3:23). Not only are we dead in our sin, but the Scriptures tell us that we are God's enemies. We are not merely indifferent to him. By nature, we hate him (Eph. 2:1–3). But what does Paul tell us elsewhere? He writes: "For if while we were enemies we were reconciled to God by the death of his Son, much more, now that we are reconciled, shall we be saved by his life" (Rom. 5:10). In other words, what we were powerless to do, God accomplished in Christ. God has condescended into this sin-darkened world and put forth his only Son as a costly sacrifice that we might be saved, lifted out of the miry depths, and raised from death to life. If God has done this in Christ, that which we were utterly incapable of doing, then why would we ever use our God-given freedom to return to the bondage from which he has delivered us?

I believe a source of our legalism originates in the way we read our Bibles, particularly the Old Testament: we fail to see Christ. We read the law, for example, as if Christ never came. When we read the Scriptures, especially the Old Testament, we must do so looking for Christ. Jesus himself taught his disciples that he is the interpretive key to the Old Testament. Jesus explained everything concerning his own ministry, Luke tells us, from the "Law of Moses and the Prophets and the Psalms" (Luke 24:44–45), which is another way of saying, the whole Old Testament.

This is something that the church has historically always done. Nevertheless, John Calvin's words are quite helpful:

> We must hold that Christ cannot be properly known from anywhere but the Scriptures. And if that is so, it follows that the Scriptures should be read with the aim of finding Christ in them. Whoever turns aside from this object, even though he wears himself out all his life in learning, will never reach the knowledge of the truth. . . . For Christ did not first begin to be manifested in the Gospel; but the one to whom the Law and the Prophets bore witness was openly revealed in the Gospel.[3]

3. John Calvin, *John 1–10*, CNTC, trans. T. H. L. Parker, eds. David W. Torrance and T. F. Torrance (Grand Rapids, MI: Eerdmans, [1961] 1995), 139.

If we can understand this point, then our study of the Scriptures will reveal Christ as the central focus.

This was the precise problem for the Jews in Christ's day: "But their minds were hardened. For to this day, when they read the old covenant, that same veil remains unlifted, because only through Christ is it taken away. Yes, to this day whenever Moses is read a veil lies over their hearts" (2 Cor. 3:14–15). If we seek Christ first, we will not read the law and think that it is ours to fulfill for our salvation but instead see the righteousness of Christ in *his* fulfillment of the law. We will not read the Old Testament civil laws and think that they are for the civil government today, but we will recognize that they foreshadow the righteousness of the kingdom of Christ. We will not read of the Old Testament sacrifices and think that there is something that we ourselves can do to somehow earn God's favor, but instead recognize that Christ is our perfect sacrifice. In this way, then, we will see the person of Christ standing upon our horizon and will recognize him, and him alone, as both the author and finisher of our faith.

I hope we see not only in Paul's letter to the Galatians, but throughout the whole of the Scriptures, the person and work of Jesus Christ as the center of Scripture. If we see and recognize that Jesus is the fulfillment of all of God's promises, and that we no longer dwell in the shadowlands but stand in the light of his revelation, we will never want to turn back the clock. We will recognize that it is only through our union with Christ by faith that we can be justified, sanctified, and glorified. We will not try to bring our paltry offerings before God's throne in an attempt to earn his favor. Instead, we will bring the perfect righteousness of Jesus Christ, knowing that he has secured God's favor.

This section of Galatians also contains a telltale warning to all Christians. Paul exhorted the Galatians not to return to their former ways. This is not simply a temptation for first-century

Christians but one that faces all Christians. Even for those who have never known a day apart from Christ and have been raised in Christian homes, there is the temptation to wander away from the path of righteousness, to dally with sin. Like an alcoholic who has been dry and on the wagon for a number of years but then stops in the parking lot of a bar and lingers, all too often Christians can look wistfully at their former pre-Christian lives. They remember the "fun" and "freedom" they had. Like the alcoholic who promises to have just one sip that turns into just one drink that turns into yet another drunken bender, our own dalliances with sin can easily escalate from the seemingly harmless to the soul-threatening.

Regardless of the nature of the temptation, Christians should always steer clear and seek Christ. We must remember that however attractive our former lives appear, our sinful past is a whitewashed tomb—the outside looks clean but the inside is filled with death. Only Christ through the Spirit and his Word can keep our thinking straight and affix our desires upon that which is holy and pure. Therefore, we must always flee sin and diligently pursue Christ.

13

Christ Formed in You

GALATIANS 4:12–20

Have I then become your enemy by telling you the truth? They make much of you, but for no good purpose. They want to shut you out, that you may make much of them. It is always good to be made much of for a good purpose, and not only when I am present with you, my little children, for whom I am again in the anguish of childbirth until Christ is formed in you! I wish I could be present with you now and change my tone, for I am perplexed about you.

Since the middle of the second chapter, Paul has been busily engaged in theological argumentation in his efforts to reclaim the Galatian churches for the gospel. He has employed the Old Testament expansively to show how the gospel that he preached to the Galatian churches was the truth. Not only has Paul cited specific passages of Old Testament Scripture, such as Deuteronomy 27:26, Leviticus 18:5, and Genesis 15:6, but he has also employed the Exodus narrative to characterize the nature of the freedom that the gospel of Christ brings. Israel was imprisoned by the law, enslaved to it, and under its curse. Likewise, the Gentiles were imprisoned under false teaching and vain philosophy. Both Jews and Gentiles were imprisoned by the elemental principles of the world. Yet Jesus Christ came and delivered both from the curse of the law so that they might enjoy the freedom of life in the Spirit. God freed them, not by their works of obedience but by the obedience of Jesus. Salvation and justification were by faith, not by works.

At this stage in Paul's letter, we find a brief respite from Paul's theological argumentation and, as in the beginning of this epistle, he personally engages the Galatians. He draws attention to his own conduct among them. We also find some very personal statements by the apostle that give us some insights into his own struggles. In the end, however, Paul's personal references culminate, not in an exaltation of self, but rather the self-sacrificing character of his ministry. What was the goal of his ministry? It was to see Christ formed in the Galatian Christians. Indeed, it is this goal—Christ formed in His people—that should be the desire and goal of every minister of the gospel.

Become as Paul

First, Paul exhorts the Galatians to become like him: "Brothers, I entreat you, become as I am, for I also have become as you are. You did me no wrong" (Gal. 4:12). When Paul calls upon the Galatians to become like him, he is not saying that they should imitate his personality or dress. Rather, in the overall context, he entreats the Galatians to become as he is in their relationship to the law.

In order to bring the gospel to the Gentiles, Paul became as a Gentile—he was willing, for example, to eat with them and consume their food, which would have been a big problem for a Jew who observed the dietary laws. Paul elsewhere addressed his willingness to adapt to whatever context he found himself in, whether among Jews or Gentiles: "For though I am free from all, I have made myself a servant to all, that I might win more of them. To the Jews I became as a Jew, in order to win Jews. To those under the law I became as one under the law (though not being myself under the law) that I might win those under the law" (1 Cor. 9:19–20). Paul was willing to adapt external things (e.g., his diet and dress) to the expectations of the people around him so as not to offend them. This way, they could focus on the gospel rather than a perceived offense. By being mindful of Jewish dietary sensitivities in some contexts and Gentile concerns in others, the apostle allowed the gospel to stand out, not what type of food he ate. Paul therefore was encouraging the Galatians to leave behind the bondage of the law and to become as he was—one who was free in Christ.

Paul's Personal Testimony

Paul opens up to the Galatians in a very personal way: "You know it was because of a bodily ailment that I preached the gospel to you at first, and though my condition was a trial to you, you did not scorn or despise me, but received me as an angel of God, as Christ Jesus. What then has become of the blessing you felt? For I testify to you that, if possible, you would have gouged out your eyes and given them to me" (Gal. 4:13–15). Paul draws attention to the kindness that the Galatians first showed him when he arrived to preach the gospel. Paul does not go into great detail about his infirmity. He explains that he had a "bodily ailment," that his condition was "a trial" to the Galatians, and that the Galatians would have gladly given him their very own eyes. So, it seems from this information that Paul suffered from some sort of eye malady. Nevertheless, we should not get distracted by the exact nature of Paul's ailment but instead focus upon his weakness and the Galatian response.

The Galatians did not scorn or despise him, but instead, they treated him as though he were an angel or even Jesus himself. Paul wonders why they would turn against him now, if indeed, this was the nature of their relationship—one characterized by kindness and love. "Have I then become your enemy by telling you the truth?" (Gal. 4:16). In other words, Paul's care and love for the Galatians has not changed, and for this reason he has strenuously labored to show them the truth. By contrast, the false teachers were not interested in the truth: "They make much of you, but for no good purpose. They want to shut you out, that you may make much of them" (Gal. 4:17). Paul explains that the false teachers were taking advantage of the Galatians. They were filled with false praise for them. Additionally, Paul explains that they "shut you out," which means that they wanted to isolate the Galatians from all other influences, especially the apostle himself. Again, what was the purpose of isolating them? It was so that the Galatians would look exclusively to the false teachers—and thus the false teachers could keep the Galatian churches under their influence.

Paul goes on to write: "It is always good to be made much of for a good purpose, and not only when I am present with you, my little children, for whom I am again in the anguish of childbirth until Christ is formed in you" (Gal. 4:18–19). It is one thing for a teacher or preacher to put his congregation front-and-center, if for a good purpose, such as praising the work of God in them. Paul has done this in his ministry (2 Cor. 3:1–4). Nevertheless, the apostle knew this was not the case with the false teachers—the Judaizers did not have the glory of God or the edification of the church in mind: they only had their own selfish interests at heart.

A window into the apostle's heart also appears as he calls the Galatians his "little children." We might read Paul's letter to the Galatians and think that he is quite angry and only interested in right doctrine, in orthodoxy, and cares little, if anything, for the people. Such a conclusion, however, would be a severe misreading of the letter. Paul was deeply concerned for the Galatians. He is like a concerned parent who sees his child in imminent danger. His passion is driven by love and concern for the people, not simply a detached veneration of doctrinal orthodoxy. This is the source of his agitation, but it is ultimately evidence of Paul's great concern and love for the Galatians.

Indeed, the apostle's love is evident not only because he calls them his "little children" but also because he was again in the anguish of childbirth to see Christ formed in them. There are distinct differences between Paul and the false teachers. The false teachers isolated the Galatians for their own selfish benefits whereas Paul pointed them to Christ and desired to see Christ formed in them. In the last verse of this section, the apostle expresses more of his affection for the Galatians as well as perhaps some of his continued frustration: "I wish I could be present with you now and change my tone, for I am perplexed about you" (Gal. 4:20). In person, Paul might have moderated his tone, but nevertheless, he was still concerned and frustrated over the fact that the Galatians had embraced this false gospel.

Much of what Paul writes revolves around his relationship with the Galatians—the relationship between a pastor and his congregation. We can further divide our observations in terms of the pastor's responsibility towards his sheep and the congregation's responsibility to the pastor.

The Pastor's Responsibility to His Sheep

It should be evident from what Paul has written that a pastor is merely a conduit, if you will, for the Lord Jesus. A conduit is a means by which something is transmitted. What does the pastor transmit to his congregation? The pastor must transmit Christ. When the Westminster divines originally composed their Confession of Faith, they also wrote a Directory for Public Worship. In its instructions for the preacher, the Directory calls him to preach "faithfully, looking at the honor of Christ, the conversion, edification, and salvation of the people, not at his own gain or glory; keeping nothing back which may promote those holy ends, giving to every one his own portion, and bearing indifferent respect unto all, without neglecting the meanest, or sparing the greatest, in their sins."[1] In other words, the preacher always points to Christ and never himself. Whether through the preaching and teaching of the Word or the administration of the sacraments, the pastor must be a conduit for Christ. If a pastor is truly a conduit for Christ, then he will be self-effacing and humble. The pastor cannot be interested in gathering a group of disciples or establishing himself as the sole or exclusive influence in the life of his congregation.

Even pastors who genuinely love Christ but are severely misled in their thinking may attempt to "protect their flock" from outside influence, only to discover that their own influence has obscured Christ's. But selfless service that points to Christ alone is even more antithetical to the thought of false teachers. Remember that the Judaizers in Galatia, in order to exercise a self-serving, exclusive influence over the Galatian churches, sought to isolate them from Paul. The false teachers were seeking their own benefit rather than the benefit of the body, the church. Paul testifies to this fact towards the conclusion of his letter: "It is those who want to make a good showing in the flesh who would force you to be circumcised, and only in order that they may not be persecuted for the cross of Christ" (Gal. 6:12). Paul, on the other hand, was not interested in cloning himself—in seeing others duplicate his own personal life and actions. He was interested in self-duplication only to the degree that Christ was formed in the Galatians. In other words, Paul did not want the Galatians walking in lockstep with him on every single issue. He did, however, want the Galatians to follow

1. *Directory for Public Worship*, in *Westminster Confession of Faith* (Glasgow: Free Presbyterian Publications, [1648] 1995), 381.

him as he followed Christ. He wanted them to become like him in forsaking the bondage of the law. Again, he wanted to see Christ formed in them.

The bottom line is that the role of a pastor is to point beyond himself to Christ. The desire and conduct of a pastor must emulate John the Baptist who said, "He must increase but I must decrease" (John 3:30). Only Christ can equip and enable the pastor to do this, because every person, (and this includes every pastor), faces a strong foe—his own ego. A well-known minister's prayer aptly captures the heart of a godly minister, one that expresses the need for unction and self-effacement:

> My master God,
> I am desired to preach today,
> but go weak and needy to my task;
> Yet I long that people might be edified with divine truth,
> that an honest testimony might be borne of thee;
> Give me assistance in preaching and prayer,
> with heart uplifted for grace and unction.
> Present to my view things pertinent to my subject,
> with fullness of matter and clarity of thought,
> proper expressions, fluency, fervency,
> a feeling sense of the things I preach,
> and grace to apply them to men's consciences.
> Keep me conscious all the while of my defects
> and let me not gloat in pride over my performance. . . .
> I myself need thy support, comfort, strength, holiness,
> that I might be a pure channel of thy grace,
> and be able to do something for thee; . . .
> keep me in tune with thee as I do this work.[2]

This type of sentiment should mark not only ministers but also churches. Therefore, churches should pray that the Lord would equip and enable pastors to point beyond themselves to Christ.

2. "A Minister's Preaching," in *The Valley of Vision*, ed. Arthur Bennett (Edinburgh: Banner of Truth, [1975] 2007), 348–349.

But if a minister's goal is to set forth Christ, then this means that he should, with Paul, desire to see Christ formed in his congregation. Some pastors look upon their congregations as a nuisance—the people that interrupt his study time. Others look at their congregants as walking problems—after a while, a pastor can grow weary of dealing with the problems in his congregation. He grows cynical and does not see people for whom Christ died but only the counseling problems they represent. How many pastors pray and intercede for the people in their churches? Paul was in the anguish of childbirth until Christ was formed in the Galatians. All ministers of the gospel should be equally concerned for their own flocks.

This means not only praying for the church, but also preaching the gospel faithfully. Gospel ministry also involves discipleship: visiting with church members and holding them accountable to their baptisms and professions of faith—to honor the name that they bear. All too often, pastors may pray and preach, but they won't personally confront the sin they see in the members of their church—they turn a blind eye to conduct or doctrine that contradicts the Word of God. If we learn anything from Galatians, it is that Paul's love for the Galatians was not at all contrary to his willingness to confront them with their sin.

The Congregation's Responsibility to the Pastor

Though Paul had to rebuke the Galatian churches for their error, he yet commended them for the way they had received him initially. In particular, two things stand out. First, the Galatians were sacrificial and loving. So often, when people see weakness in others, they shun or ridicule them. This was not at all how the Galatians treated Paul. While he suffered from his eye ailment, the Galatians received him warmly, and even responded sacrificially to his need. Paul says that they would have even given him their eyes if it were possible. This conduct is certainly exemplary and gives us an idea of how a congregation should treat its pastor. Far too many pastors are forced to eke out a meager financial existence while the church could afford to pay him more. Far too many congregations expect their pastors to sacrifice his time, money, and resources but are unwilling to sacrifice for him. Yet the very nature of sacrifice tells us that it is costly and even painful—such is the conduct that marked the Galatians towards Paul, and such is the conduct that should mark any church that is redeemed by Christ and indwelled by the Holy Spirit.

Second, the churches of Galatia not only loved Paul, but they received him as an angel of God, even as Christ Jesus himself. This does not mean that they worshipped Paul. Rather, think of this conduct in light of what he has said. If the pastor points beyond himself to Christ, then the congregation should recognize him for what he is—a conduit for Christ. In this way, they should receive his teaching and preaching as they would the words of Christ. This does not negate the need to be good Bereans (Acts 17:10–11), but how many come to church to hear Christ speak in the preaching and teaching of the Word? Or how many come only to hear a talk or lecture? Historically, the Reformed tradition has placed a great premium upon the preaching of the Word. For example, *The Second Helvetic Confession* (1566), written by first-generation Reformer Heinrich Bullinger (1504–1575), states: "Wherefore when this Word of God is now preached in the church by preachers lawfully called, we believe that the very Word of God is preached, and received by the faithful."[3]

At the same time, the congregation must receive the pastor as Christ himself in the way that they would receive any other member of the body of Christ. Each member of the church has been redeemed by the precious blood of Christ and incor-

---

3. *The Second Helvetic Confession* 1.4 in *Reformed Confessions Harmonized: With an Annotated Bibliography of Reformed Doctrinal Works*, eds. Joel R. Beeke and Sinclair B. Ferguson (Grand Rapids, MI: Baker, 1999), 12.

porated into his body. This means that we must receive one another as Christ himself, and that we must love one another as though we were demonstrating our love to Christ himself (Matt. 25:35–40). Once again, only Christ can create within us the ability to love one another in this Christ-like manner. This was at the heart of Paul's instruction—namely, seeking Christ and salvation by faith rather than by the works of the law. In other words, only the power of the Holy Spirit working through faith can create these abilities in us, not our own obedience to the law.

In a sense, we have been given a respite from Paul's relentless assault upon the false teaching of the Judaizers. In the midst of the calm, however, as the smoke lifts from the battlefield, we find a mutually edifying and loving relationship between a pastor and his congregation. It is a relationship that is founded in Christ and the Holy Spirit. The Galatian abandonment of the gospel, however, struck at this foundation, putting the relationship in mortal danger.

14

Sarah and Hagar

GALATIANS 4:21–31

Now you, brothers, like Isaac, are children of promise. But just as at that time he who was born according to the flesh persecuted him who was born according to the Spirit, so also it is now. But what does the Scripture say? "Cast out the slave woman and her son, for the son of the slave woman shall not inherit with the son of the free woman." So, brothers, we are not children of the slave but of the free woman.

In a heated argument, two people can completely forget what they were arguing about. As the volume, heat, and intensity rise, people become interested in refuting the previous statement and the argument can drift far away from its original cause. What began as a disagreement over what color a room should be painted turns into an argument about how rude a person is—people forget all about the color of the room. Something like this alters the arguments of the false teachers at Galatia. They were so vigorously intent on making the Gentile converts submit to circumcision that they failed to give careful attention to what the Old Testament Scriptures had to say about subjects such as justification. They were so intent on following the law that they forgot altogether what the law had to say. Paul was all too willing to correct their faulty memories. Hence, in the passage before us, Paul returns to the Old Testament to continue building his argument. In particular, he illustrates the difference between the Judaizers' false gospel (which relied on our obedience to the law), and the true gospel (resting on Christ's obedience received through faith) by invoking the Old Testament figures of Sarah and Hagar.

Listening to the Old Testament

Paul begins this section of chapter 4 by asking the Galatians a significant question: "Tell me, you who desire to be under the law, do you not listen to the law?" (Gal. 4:21) He asks the Judaizers why they desire to be under the bondage of law, when it seems as though they have paid little, if any attention to what the law actually says. Paul uses the term *law* in two different senses. The first occurrence denotes the Mosaic covenant; the second refers more broadly to the first five books of the Bible, the Pentateuch. To paraphrase Paul's question: "Tell me, you who desire to be under the Mosaic covenant for your redemption, do you not listen to the first five books of the Bible which *contain* the Mosaic covenant?"

Abraham, the great patriarch, had two sons, Isaac and Ishmael (Gen. 16; 21:1–21). Paul reminds the false teachers that Ishmael was the son of the slave woman, Hagar, and that Isaac was born of Sarah, a free woman. In particular, it is important to note how Paul distinguishes their births in verse 23. Paul says that Ishmael was "born according to the flesh" while Isaac was "born through the promise." Remember that God promised to Abraham that he would give him descendants as numerous as the stars of the sky (Gen. 12:3; 15:5; 22:17–18). Time passed and Abraham was still

Sarah and Hagar

childless. So what did he and Sarah do? They took matters into their own hands. They tried to lay hold of God's covenant promise through their own sinful efforts; Sarah instructed Abraham to have sexual relations with her handmaid, Hagar (Gen. 16:3–4). That Sarah and Abraham tried to lay hold of the covenant promise through their sinful efforts is why Paul characterizes the birth of Ishmael as "according to the flesh." Notice how the apostle characterizes the works of the *flesh* in the next chapter: "Now the works of the flesh are evident: sexual immorality" (Gal. 5:19). By contrast, Paul characterizes Isaac's birth as "through the promise."

Recall that Sarah was well beyond child-bearing age, but God nevertheless blessed her and Abraham and enabled them, by his grace, to produce a son, Isaac (cf. Rom. 4:19). There is a significant contrast—one son born through sinful human effort and the other born through God's grace in fulfillment of his covenant promise. Herein lies Paul's point. Hagar, Paul says in verse 24, corresponds to Mount Sinai, which is connected to the earthly Jerusalem. Sarah, on the other hand, corresponds to the heavenly Jerusalem: "Now Hagar is Mount Sinai in Arabia; she corresponds to the present Jerusalem, for she is in slavery with her children. But the Jerusalem above is free, and she is our mother" (Gal. 4:25–26). One gives birth to slaves and the other gives birth to freemen.

Paul connects the Judaizers to the earthly Jerusalem, to Hagar, and says that they are trying to lay hold of God's covenant promises through their own sinful efforts. Rather than acquiring the blessings they so desperately seek, they enslave themselves to the law. By contrast, those who seek the blessing through faith in Christ receive the blessing of the covenant through God's faithfulness to his promise. Paul draws upon a prevalent theme in the Old Testament that reaches a fever pitch in the New Testament, and especially here in Galatians; namely, the contrast between Sinai and Zion. Mt. Zion is where God has built his sanctuary, high in the heavens (Ps. 78:68–69). Mt. Zion is the final dwelling place of the triune Lord—the city of the living God, the heavenly Jerusalem, the last temple, the temple of Christ, who is the chief cornerstone (John 2:19; Eph. 2:20; Heb. 12:22). Paul then quotes a passage from Isaiah 54:1: "For it is written, 'Rejoice, O barren one who does not bear; break forth and cry aloud, you who are not in labor! For the children of the desolate one will be more than those of the one who has a husband'" (Gal. 4:27).

In the original context, Israel was in exile because of her disobedience to the Mosaic covenant. She was like an adulterous wife. But in Isaiah 54, God promises that he will take her again as a wife and she will not be barren any longer; she will have numerous offspring. In the surrounding verses of the Isaianic passage there are hints that point backwards to God's covenant with Noah (vv. 9–10), as well as hints that point forward to the New Jerusalem (vv. 11–12)—and the passage anticipates the very architecture of the new Jerusalem in the book of Revelation (Rev. 21:16–21):

> "This is like the days of Noah to me: as I swore that the waters of Noah should no more go over the earth, so I have sworn that I will not be angry with you, and will not rebuke you. For the mountains may depart and the hills be removed, but my steadfast love shall not depart from you, and my covenant of peace shall not be removed," says the LORD, who has compassion on you. "O afflicted one, storm-tossed and not comforted, behold, I will set your stones in antimony, and lay your foundations with sapphires. I will make your pinnacles of agate, your gates of carbuncles, and all your wall of precious stones. All your children shall be taught by the LORD, and great shall be the peace of your children." (Isaiah 54:9–13)

Sarah and Hagar

Even Paul's appeal to this portion of Israel's history fits within his argument: Israel, through her attempt to render obedience to the Lord, has merited only exile and curse. By contrast, in spite of Israel's disobedience, God by his grace will nevertheless redeem his people—he will fulfill his covenant promise. And more to the point of the quotation, the children of the promise, those who look to Christ by faith, through the power of the Holy Spirit, will outnumber those who seek their redemption through obedience to the law.

Paul goes on to explain that the Genesis narratives about Abraham reveal even more about the nature of God's covenant promises: "Now you, brothers, like Isaac, are children of promise. But just as at that time he who was born according to the flesh persecuted him who was born according to the Spirit, so also it is now" (Gal. 4:28–29). Paul looks back to the narrative and reminds us first of our identity. We, the church, are like Isaac; we are children of the promise because we are born, not through flesh and blood, nor the will of a father, nor by human decision, but by the Holy Spirit (John 1:11–13).

Paul explains that Ishmael, the slave child, the child born according to the flesh, persecuted Isaac, the free child born according to the promise. We read about this persecution in Genesis 21:8–9: "And the child grew and was weaned. And Abraham made a great feast on the day that Isaac was weaned. But Sarah saw the son of Hagar the Egyptian, whom she had borne to Abraham, laughing." At first glance, this might seem insignificant, but we should understand that the term *laughing* here means "to make sport of," or "to toy with." Ishmael, therefore, was *ridiculing* Isaac. If we read between the lines, Ishmael might have been making fun of the "unique" circumstances surrounding Isaac's conception—that is, he was born to Sarah and Abraham long after their childbearing years. However, to ridicule his unique conception was, in effect, to ridicule God's faithfulness to his promise.

Paul then quotes Genesis 21:10 to draw attention to what happened to Hagar and Ishmael: "But what does the Scripture say? 'Cast out the slave woman and her son, for the son of the slave woman shall not inherit with the son of the free woman'" (Gal. 4:30). Paul emphatically makes his point that the child of Hagar, Ishmael, and all those who seek redemption through their own sinful efforts will in no way partake of the covenant blessings which are reserved for the children of promise. Instead, they will be cast out of the covenant community, which was precisely what happened to Hagar and Ishmael. In contrast, Paul reminds the Galatians: "So, brothers, we are not children of the slave but of the free woman" (Gal. 4:31). In other words, those who look to Christ by faith are children of the promise, for they have been born, not of sinful human effort but by the grace of God through the work of the Holy Spirit. Salvation and justification come by God's grace alone.

The Prevalence of Works-Righteousness

In all of the other religions of the world, man is required to do something in order to earn his salvation. He is required to offer his life, make sacrifices, surrender his possessions, give to others, commit acts of kindness, deny his own evil desires, or whatever the case may be. This tendency certainly found its way into Old Testament Israel and then of course the churches of Galatia. In Israel, before the covenant at Sinai, Abraham and Sarah thought they could lay hold of God's covenant promise by their own sinful efforts. This pattern found its way into Abraham's offspring. Think, for example, of Jacob, who tried to lay hold of the covenant blessing through his deception and knavery (Gen. 27). It was not until God, the pre-incarnate Christ, wrestled with Jacob in the wilderness and disabled him that he realized that it was only by God's mercy that he could obtain the covenant blessing, not through his sinful efforts (Gen. 32:22–32). Many in Israel thought that by circumcision or by sacrifices they could somehow make themselves fit for God.

This works-righteousness mindset is perhaps best illustrated by the rich young ruler who asked Jesus what must he do to inherit eternal life (Luke 18:18ff). Paul's answer to this question undoubtedly comes as a shock—the sinful person cannot *do* anything. Rather, the sinful person must look by faith to what another has done on his behalf. In terms of the big question of our salvation, if I may modify a saying made popular by a former president: "Ask not what you can do for your God, but rather what God has done for you in Christ." This was the fundamental point that the Judaizers missed.

Moreover, this is the fundamental point that so many in our day, even within the church, fail to see. But this is the precise nature of the gospel: "If, because of one man's trespass, death reigned through that one man, much more will those who receive the abundance of grace and the free gift of righteousness reign in life through the one man Jesus Christ" (Rom. 5:17). In fact, in our own day, even as in Paul's day, the common response is one of unbelief! How can God require nothing in terms of man's own obedience? Would not such a free redemption lead to rampant lawlessness? Paul had to address this very question: "What shall we say then? Are we to continue in sin that grace may abound? By no means! How can we who died to sin still live in it?" (Rom. 6:1–2). We will see in the sections to come that lawlessness does not reign in those who have been redeemed by God's grace through faith alone in Christ alone.

Our role in salvation is primarily passive. Indeed, we are *objects* of God's sovereign mercy and grace! The Bible describes us as being dead in our sins and trespasses. Dead people can do nothing. God, in his mercy, reaches down and brings us out of spiritual death into life by the power of the Holy Spirit. He removes our heart of stone, unstops our ears, removes the scales from our eyes, and enables us to see, hear, and believe in the Lord Jesus Christ. Our faith is *extraspective*: we look to another for our salvation, to his life, death, resurrection, and ascension. We can find peace only in the work of Christ.

But just because we are passive in our salvation as the recipients of God's grace does not mean that we are to be inactive in our Christian lives. As Christians, we have been freed from slavery to serve Christ in righteousness. As Paul elsewhere writes: "Do not present your members to sin as instruments for unrighteousness, but present yourselves to God as those who have been brought from death to life, and your members to God as instruments for righteousness" (Rom. 6:13). Hence, as children of the promise, we should live accordingly. All too often as Christians we forget our royal identity as children of the free woman. Like the prodigal, we wallow in the mud with the swine. As children of the free woman, we should neither desire to return to the slavery of sin nor should we cast aside our rights and privileges as the adopted sons of God. Instead, our conduct should befit our royal status, a status given to us by God's grace in Christ.

15

Freedom in Christ

GALATIANS 5:1–6

You are severed from Christ, you who would be justified by the law; you have fallen away from grace. For through the Spirit, by faith, we ourselves eagerly wait for the hope of righteousness. For in Christ Jesus neither circumcision nor uncircumcision counts for anything, but only faith working through love.

In the previous chapter, Paul contrasted a false approach to salvation (that of works) with the one true approach—faith. To illustrate the differences, he returned to the Genesis narratives surrounding God's covenant promises to Abraham. Abraham and Sarah heard the covenant promise, but then tried by their own sinful efforts to lay hold of the fulfillment of that promise. Abraham listened to Sarah and impregnated her handmaid, Hagar, who produced a son, Ishmael. This was not the child of the promise that God had covenanted to give to Abraham. By contrast, when Abraham and Sarah looked to the Lord by faith, he granted them the child of the covenant promise, and Isaac was born. Ishmael was not the child of the promise, but Isaac was. Ishmael was the fruit of Abraham and Sarah's sinful efforts and scheming, whereas Isaac was the fruit of their faith in the Lord's covenant promise. Subsequently, Ishmael persecuted Isaac, and so Sarah had Abraham cast out Ishmael and Hagar from their midst. Paul drew our attention to the fact that Ishmael was the son of a slave, Hagar, whereas Isaac, the heir of the covenant promise, was the son of a free woman, Sarah.

Paul connected these events to his situation in Galatia and identified those who sinfully sought to obtain their salvation through faith *and* works as the children of Hagar, the children of the earthly Jerusalem. By contrast, he connected those who sought salvation and justification by faith alone in Christ as the children of Sarah, the free woman, the children of the heavenly Jerusalem. Paul concluded the chapter and his use of the Old Testament with the following words: "So, brothers, we are not children of the slave but of the free woman" (Gal. 4:31). In other words, seeking salvation through obedience to the law merits only the curse and bondage of the law. Seeking salvation by faith alone in Christ, on the other hand, brings freedom.

Paul moves forward to explain both the bondage of the law and freedom from it. These are important points that we must grasp. In other words, for the Christian, what does it mean to be freed from the bondage of the law? Does it mean we are free to do as we please? Are we free to sin because God has freed us from the bondage and curse of the law in Christ? The quick answer, of course, is absolutely not.

Returning to the Bondage and Curse of the Law

Paul begins the chapter by reiterating the point he has made in chapter 4 with the appeal to the Abrahamic narratives surrounding the births of Ishmael and Isaac: "For freedom Christ has set us free; stand firm therefore, and do not submit again to a yoke of slavery" (Gal. 5:1). Paul exhorts the Galatians to recognize the freedom they have in Christ and to stand firm in that freedom. Christ rendered perfect obedience to the law on behalf of those who look to him by faith. Christ suffered the curse of the law on behalf of those who look to him by faith (Gal. 3:13). To return to the law as a means of one's salvation is to return to a yoke of slavery. Or to put it into the terms of Israel's Old Testament narrative history, it is like Israel wanting to return to the slavery of Egypt after they had been delivered miraculously through the Red Sea.

Paul continues to explain the nature of justification by faith alone by showing the Galatians the mutually exclusive relationship between faith and works: "Look: I, Paul, say to you that if you accept circumcision, Christ will be of no advantage to you. I testify again to every man who accepts circumcision that he is obligated to keep the whole law. You are severed from Christ, you who would be justified by the law; you have fallen away from grace" (Gal. 5:2–4). There are two paths to justification—one through perfect obedience to the law and the other by faith alone in Christ alone. The two paths are mutually exclusive. If a person seeks justification and salvation through his obedience, then the perfect obedience of Christ is of no avail. Our salvation is not a joint enterprise between us and God where he provides a little bit of help and then we do the best we can. On the contrary, to attempt to bring forward our obedience (even at one point of the law), as grounds for our justification, is to bring upon ourselves the obligation to obey the entirety of the law.

But because of the original sin of Adam, we have inherited the guilt of his sin as well as its corruption. And because we are given to sin, our own personal sins weigh us down. All we need is one single solitary sin and the weight of the entire the law and its attending curse come crashing down upon us like a tidal wave. Paul goes on to state the antithesis in even starker terms by telling the Galatians that if they seek to be justified by their obedience to the law, then they are severed from Christ and they have fallen from grace. We should note Paul's subtle wordplay here. The false teachers were forcing others to be circumcised in order to be saved, which involved the severing of the foreskin. But in submitting to circumcision for one's justification and salvation, the person not only severed his foreskin from his body but also severed himself from Christ. In not so many words, Paul is saying that by seeking salvation through circumcision, they instead receive the curse of the covenant, for to be severed from Christ is to be severed from the blessings of the Abrahamic covenant.

We should note, additionally, that when Paul writes, "You are severed from Christ, you who would be justified by the law; you have fallen away from grace" (Gal. 5:4), he does not mean that a person can lose his salvation. If this were the case, then Paul would contradict himself with what he writes elsewhere, namely that there is nothing that can separate us from the love of God in Christ (Rom. 8:31–35). Rather, Paul states that anyone within the visible body of Christ who seeks to be justified from the law is actually severed from Christ. The person who seeks to be justified by his works, in reality, has fallen from the grace that he has tried to obtain. Like a child who stands on a stool to reach a high object but then loses his balance and falls off, so the person who tries to ascend to heaven by his works will inevitably fall back to earth because the weight of his sin and the curse of the law are too heavy for any sinner to overcome.

The Nature of Salvation by Faith Alone in Christ Alone

What, then, does Paul have to say about the other way of salvation? What does he have to write about salvation by faith alone in Christ alone? Paul explains: "For through the Spirit, by faith, we ourselves eagerly wait for the hope of righteousness" (Gal.

5:5). Notice immediately the contrast between salvation by works versus faith. The Judaizers sought salvation through the flesh, literally, whereas Paul writes that salvation is "through the Spirit, by faith." Paul continues to build up to what will follow in chapter five concerning the antithesis between the "flesh" and the "Spirit" (i.e., the works of the flesh contrasted with the fruit of the Spirit). Nevertheless, the priority Paul places upon the sovereignty of God in salvation is evident.

The regenerative life-giving work of the Spirit imparts salvation. Our redemption is extraspective in character because we look by faith to the work of another, Jesus Christ. Those who look to Christ by faith, those who have been justified by faith alone, eagerly look forward to the hope of righteousness, the hope of the completion of their salvation. They look forward to the completion of their sanctification and their glorification—the enrobing in the glorified, resurrected, and perfectly sanctified body—to be clothed in immortality (2 Cor. 5:1–4). As William Perkins explains the nature of Paul's expression, "we ourselves eagerly wait for the hope of righteousness" (Gal. 5:5): "Faith apprehends the promise, and thereby brings forth hope: and faith by means of hope, makes them that believe to wait." But what of the "hope of righteousness"? Perkins writes:

> That is, salvation or life eternal, which is the fruit of righteousness (Titus 2:13) or again, righteousness hoped for. Righteousness indeed is imputed to them that believe, and that in this life, yet the fruition and the full revelation thereof is reserved to the life to come, when Christ our righteousness shall appear, and when the effect of righteousness, namely sanctification, shall be accomplished in us (Rom. 8:23; 1 John 3:2).[1]

---

1. William Perkins, *A Commentary on Galatians*, ed. Gerald T. Shepherd (New York: Pilgrim Press, [1617] 1989), 334.

What the false teachers sought by their corrupted works, the people of God seek and obtain instead by faith alone in Christ alone through the power of the Holy Spirit: eternal life itself.

Paul explains: "For in Christ Jesus neither circumcision nor uncircumcision counts for anything, but only faith working through love" (Gal. 5:6). Paul once again reminds the Galatians that, concerning salvation, circumcision or uncircumcision was immaterial. Within the broader context of Galatians, Paul is saying that whether one was a Jew (circumcised) or a Gentile (uncircumcised), obedience to the law or racial identity counts for nothing. Faith alone in Christ alone brings salvation and justification. And faith produces the fruit of love, or as Paul states it, "faith working through love." In other words, once a person is justified by faith alone, he does not attempt to return to the bondage of the law but instead seeks to manifest the love of Christ, which is the fruit of justifying faith.

John Calvin explains the nature of the relationship between faith, works, and justification. He does so by engaging the errors of the Roman Catholic Church who enlisted Galatians 5:6, specifically Paul's phrase, "faith working through love," to say that good works were necessary for a person's justification. Calvin writes:

> When they want to refute our doctrine that we are justified by faith alone, they seize up this weapon: "If the faith that justifies us be that which works by love, faith alone does not justify." I reply: they do not understand their own babbling; far less what we teach. It is not our doctrine that the faith which justifies is alone. We maintain that it is always joined with good works. But we contend that faith avails by itself for justification. The Papists themselves, like murderers, tear faith to pieces, sometimes making it *informis* [unformed] and empty of love, and sometimes *formata* [formed by love]. But we deny

that true faith can be separated from the Spirit of regeneration [sanctification]. When we debate justification, however, we exclude all works. . . . When you discuss justification, beware of allowing any mention of love or of works, but resolutely hold on to the exclusive adverb.[2]

Hence, faith does produce love, yet we are not justified on account of our love, but rather, on account of Christ's love for and obedience to the Father, which is imputed to us by faith. To claim that we are justified by faith working through love turns Paul's entire epistle on its head and argues for the very thing that the apostle manifestly denies.

Faith Working Through Love

I hope that we see the different ends of each path, namely the paths of justification by works versus justification by faith alone in Christ alone. The former severs a person from the salvation that comes only through Jesus Christ. The latter fills a person with the hope of righteousness, the hope that Christ will complete the good work that he has begun in the believer. Justification by grace alone through faith alone in Christ alone results in the complete and total salvation of the believer. Perkins again helpfully explains:

> Justification and sanctification are two distinct benefits (1 Cor. 1:30 and 6:11). Justification ministers unto us deliverance from hell, and a right to life everlasting. Sanctification is a fruit of the former, and serves to make us thankful to God for our justification: and love serves the same use, because it is a special part of sanctification.[3]

---

2. John Calvin, *Galatians, Ephesians, Philippians, and Colossians*, CNTC, trans. T. H. L. Parker, eds. David W. Torrance and T. F. Torrance (Grand Rapids, MI: Eerdmans, [1965] 1996), 96.

3. Perkins, *Galatians*, 339.

This, of course, is something in which we should all rejoice. We must preach this message to our hearts constantly.

How many of us have ever labored under the misunderstanding that we had to please God by our obedience so that we might be saved? How many of us have labored under the misunderstanding that if we sin, we can somehow lose our salvation? How many of us have ever thought ourselves to be better than others because we believed that we were more obedient? Yet all of these false opinions are built upon the Galatian heresy—beginning with the grace of God and trying to finish our salvation by our own power. A dedication to such an approach only results in condemnation, being severed from Christ. By contrast, the one who looks to Christ and trusts in his work receives the hope of righteousness. Paul is building up to an important theme in his epistle, namely the conduct that is supposed to characterize all Christians as they await the completion of their redemption. The Christian is not supposed to be marked by the works of the flesh but by faith working through love.

We should note, however, that the Christian does not use his freedom from the curse of the law—his freedom in Christ—as a license for sin. Responding to the disbelief in the utterly free nature of the grace of God in the gospel, Paul writes that believers are freed from sin, not so they can return back to the enslaving power of sin, but so they can be slaves of righteousness (Rom. 6:17–18). The believer leads this type of life until the very end: "But now that you have been set free from sin and have become slaves of God, the fruit you get leads to sanctification and its end, eternal life" (Rom. 6:22). The believer draws near to Christ through the reading and preaching of the Word—not by an idle listening or reading, mind you, but by being both a "hearer" and "doer" of the Word (James 1:23–25). Another means by which the Christian seeks conformity to Christ is through diligent and fervent prayer. In prayer, we wrestle with our sin and plead with our Savior to deliver us from its destructive power. It should go without saying that the Christian, like Joseph fleeing from Potipher's adulterous wife, should flee from all sinful conduct. Once again, the normative (or third) use of the law guides the Christian and instructs him in identifying sinful conduct.

In subsequent sections, we will see in greater detail some of the specific conduct that should mark justified sinners. However, we would be remiss if we did not pose the following question: Do we use our justification by faith alone as license to sin, to engage in the very things for which Christ paid the penalty? Or can we say that we pursue faith working through love? Keep in mind that we must define love, not as the world defines it—as some amorphous blob of warm emotion—but rather as God defines it in his Word. What are the two greatest commandments? "You shall love the Lord your God with all your heart and with all your soul and with all your mind. This is the great and first commandment" and "You shall love your neighbor as yourself" (Matt. 22:37–40). Only by seeking Christ by faith in the power of the Spirit can we live in the manner that Paul describes—faith working through love.

We can either try, unsuccessfully, to render perfect obedience to God's law, and secure for ourselves only condemnation and death, or we can look to Christ by faith in the power of the Spirit, receive our salvation as a free gift, and in that same power walk in obedience to God and in love for both God and our fellow man. Therefore, seek Christ and revel in the freedom that he has given us. Shine forth the fruit of faith by loving God and neighbor. Let us not use our God-given, Christ-wrought, Spirit-applied salvation and justification as an excuse for sin!

16

Love One Another

GALATIANS 5:7–15

For you were called to freedom, brothers. Only do not use your freedom as an opportunity for the flesh, but through love serve one another. For the whole law is fulfilled in one word: "You shall love your neighbor as yourself." But if you bite and devour one another, watch out that you are not consumed by one another.

The unbelieving world may not know much about the gospel, but it seems to understand that the church is supposed to be a place of love, kindness, and compassion. Sadly, the church can sometimes be a place devoid of love—filled with conflict, selfishness, and even hatred. Paul was keenly aware that the church should be marked by love, but understood it in a far deeper way than the unbelieving world ever could. Hence, Paul instructed the Galatians not to use their freedom in Christ as a license for sin—they were supposed to be marked by faith working through love. In other words, a justifying faith produces good works, love, and of course, the fruit of the Holy Spirit. Paul addressed this point in the previous verses (Gal. 5:1–6), but, in the verses before us, he explains how the Christian's conduct is shaped by the application of redemption. How, then, does Christ shape the life of a redeemed sinner? The answer comes through abiding in the gospel and manifesting Christ's love to others.

Paul's Concern for the Truth

Paul begins this portion of the chapter by praising the Galatians for the progress they have made: "You were running well. Who hindered you from obeying the truth?" (Gal. 5:7). Paul is pleased with the way they started but rebukes them for embracing a false gospel. To be sure, Paul reminds the Galatians that their understanding of things is mistaken: "This persuasion is not from him who calls you. A little leaven leavens the whole lump" (Gal. 5:8–9). Here he tells them that "this persuasion," their misunderstanding of the gospel, is not "from him who calls you." In other words, the false gospel is not from Jesus Christ. He then goes on to characterize the false teaching as "a little leaven."

You place a little bit of leaven in a batch of dough, and this fractional bit of leaven works its way through the entire lump of dough, causing the bread to rise when it is baked. Paul likens the Galatian heresy to leaven, implying that just a little bit of false teaching will cause evil, sin, and wickedness to work its way through all the churches of Galatia, permeating the lives of both individuals and congregations. Paul is undoubtedly concerned about the Galatians, but in the end he is confident that they will embrace the truth, and that the ultimate source of the false teaching will bear the penalty (v. 10). At the same time, Paul counters the accusation that his message has been inconsistent.

It seems from verse 11 that the false teachers had accused Paul of preaching the same gospel they were preaching: "But if I, brothers, still preach circumcision, why am I still being persecuted? In that case the offense of the cross has been re-moved" (Gal. 5:11). It seems likely that in an effort to deflect criticism away from themselves, the false teachers tried to claim Paul as one of their own. The apostle, of course, would have none of it. He asks the obvious question: If he had been preaching the necessity of circumcision, then why was he be-ing persecuted by the false teachers and those loyal to them? Notice that at the end of verse 11, Paul says that were he to preach the necessity of circumcision, then the offense of the cross would be removed. We should further unpack this oft-forgotten concept, *the offense of the cross*, as it is a prominent theme in Paul's teaching.

Paul explains in 1 Corinthians 1 that Jews demanded mirac-ulous signs and Greeks demanded demonstrations of wisdom. The cross of Christ offers neither of these things, but instead offers the crucified Savior—the incarnate God in weakness, suf-fering, and humiliation. This was a stumbling block and offense to both Jews and Greeks. They demanded more. But what does Paul say?

> For the foolishness of God is wiser than men, and the weakness of God is stronger than men. For con-sider your calling, brothers: not many of you were wise according to worldly standards, not many were powerful, not many were of noble birth. But God chose what is foolish in the world to shame the wise; God chose what is weak in the world to shame the strong; God chose what is low and despised in the world, even things that are not, to bring to nothing things that are, so that no human being might boast in the presence of God. (1 Corinthians 1:25–29)

God chose the foolish things of the world so that no one could boast in God's presence. Here, I believe, lies the offense of the cross as it relates to the Galatian heresy.

The gospel of Christ says, lay down whatever pretended righteousness and obedience you think you have and embrace the perfect righteousness and obedience of Christ. To the average Jew who thought himself to be righteous through his own obedience to the law, or in this case through his circumcision, this was an offense, a stumbling block. Paul was so insistent upon this that he uttered words that we perhaps find difficult to accept: "I wish those who unsettle you would emasculate themselves!" (Gal. 5:12). Paul was agitated enough to say, "Okay, if you are so insistent upon fulfilling the law of circumcision, I wish the knife would slip and that you would sever your member in the process."

At first glance, we might think such a statement crosses the line. But when we consider other statements from Scripture, it clearly does not. Recall Paul's conclusion in his letter to the Corinthians: "If anyone has no love for the Lord, let him be accursed" (1 Cor. 16:22). Or think of Christ's statement about those who cause children to stumble: "It would be better for him if a millstone were hung around his neck and he were cast into the sea than that he should cause one of these little ones to sin" (Luke 17:2). Moreover, while Paul is certainly employing some righteous sarcasm, at the same time, he dramatically restates the consequences of embracing a false gospel.

Remember the crisis that faced the Galatians in their abandonment of the gospel: "If anyone is preaching to you a gospel contrary to the one you received, let him be accursed" (Gal. 1:9). For one who was sensitive to the requirements of the law, Paul's statement that they should emasculate themselves would likely have been understood as one of exclusion from the covenant and the presence of God. The law states: "No one whose testicles are crushed or whose male organ is cut off shall enter the assembly of the LORD" (Deut. 23:1). Such blunt talk might seem over the top but sometimes it is pastorally necessary to awaken someone from their sin-induced stupor. Paul does not end here, however, but continues on a positive note.

Paul's Concern for Their Conduct

Paul writes: "For you were called to freedom, brothers. Only do not use your freedom as an opportunity for the flesh, but through love serve one another" (Gal. 5:13). Paul reminds the Galatians that they were called to freedom in Christ, not to return to the yoke of the bondage of the law. However, Paul did not want the Galatians to use their Christ-given freedom as an opportunity for the flesh; instead, he wanted them to be free to serve one another. What service does he have in mind? Paul writes: "For the whole law is fulfilled in one word: 'You shall love your neighbor as yourself'" (Gal. 5:14; Lev. 19:18). I think it is possible that the false teachers accused Paul of antinomianism, or lawlessness, because of his stance towards circumcision. Paul would have nothing of the sort. Rather, a person's justification leads to his sanctification, or the production of good works—the fruit of the Spirit: "Christ redeemed us from the curse of the law . . . so that we might receive the promised Spirit through faith" (Gal. 3:13–14).

Once again I think it necessary to point out the resultant ends of seeking salvation by works versus faith. Paul characterizes the "fruit" of the Galatian false gospel of works-righteousness: "But if you bite and devour one another, watch out that you are not consumed by one another" (Gal. 5:15). The pursuit of salvation by faith *and* works results in cursing, death, bondage, division, and strife. If we look to secure our standing by our works, then we will immediately begin to compare one to another and seek to establish a hierarchy, one based on our own personal achievements. Such a path automatically leads to division, strife, and self-seeking. This is why Paul warns the Galatians about devouring one another. If, on the other hand, they seek their justification and salvation by grace alone through faith alone in Christ alone, they receive the outpouring of the Spirit. The outpouring of the Spirit prompts and empowers them to love one another. Notice the absolute contrast, one that we will see in much greater detail in the following chapter: a contrast between flesh and Spirit, wickedness and love.

True Love

This passage certainly draws attention to the life-changing power of the life, death, and resurrection of Christ—the life-transforming power of the gospel. Apart from the work of Christ and the indwelling power of the Holy Spirit, we are incapable of true love. Remember, love is not some sort of warm, emotional feeling, though it can certainly involve those emotions. Rather, love is concrete, sacrificial, self-effacing service which is manifest in the ministry of Christ: his life lived for others, his death in the place of our death, his resurrection for our resurrection. We must keep the work of Christ through the Spirit in the foreground when we look to Paul's instruction that the Galatians love one another.

We are incapable of true love apart from the indwelling presence of Christ by the power of the Holy Spirit. This means we must seek the power of the Spirit in our lives through God's appointed means of grace: Word, sacraments, and prayer—so that the Spirit will conform us to the image of Christ and enable us to love. At the same time, we should be mindful of the different ways we can love our neighbor as ourselves. We should recognize that our neighbor is not only our brother or sister in Christ, but really, in the end, anyone with whom we come into contact.

Do we treat those around us with respect? Do we treat those around us as we ourselves want to be treated? Do we look out for the interests of others before our own interests?

When we hear a rumor about someone, for example, do we pass it along? Do we become a part of the problem by giving in to the desires of the flesh and cause only strife and division in the church? Take this to the next step, especially in the light of what Paul has written here. So often people disassociate correction or rebuke from love. In our modern culture a rebuke is more akin to hatred rather than love. Paul was willing to confront the sin he encountered with blunt directness. If during a routine check-up, your doctor discovered an aggressive tumor in your body that would soon kill you if left untreated, what would you want him to tell you? Would you want the doctor to look at you, smile, and say that everything was fine? Would you want the doctor to tell you not to worry, or perhaps that all you had was a cold? Anything but telling you the truth would not be a manifestation of love, but quite the opposite. What would love require?

The doctor, as uncomfortable as it might be, would have to give you the hard truth so that you could begin treatment right away. In the end, I think Paul was doing this when he told the false teachers that he wished they would emasculate themselves. That was the plain-spoken honest truth—the false teachers needed to know about the cancer that infected their hearts. Now, returning to the scenario where someone tells us a nasty rumor, how do we respond? Do we remain silent? Do we simply walk away? Or do we ask the person, in love and humility, "Please do not tell me such things." Do we go beyond and ask the question, "Does what you tell me edify the body of Christ or tear it down?" If necessary, are we willing to confront the one who gossips since they are spreading a cancer through the body of Christ? If we love one another, then, yes, that is precisely what we would do.

In the end, I hope we recognize our continued need for the gospel of Christ. Apart from the gospel of Christ, we are left to the bondage and slavery of the law. Through Christ's life, death, and resurrection, applied by the power of the Spirit, we are enabled to live, to enjoy the freedom of redemption, and the freedom to love one another. The words of the apostle John seem like a perfect way to conclude: "Beloved, let us love one another, for love is from God, and whoever loves has been born of God and knows God" (1 John 4:7).

17

Walk by the Spirit

GALATIANS 5:16–18

But I say, walk by the Spirit, and you will not gratify the desires of the flesh. For the desires of the flesh are against the Spirit, and the desires of the Spirit are against the flesh, for these are opposed to each other, to keep you from doing the things you want to do. But if you are led by the Spirit, you are not under the law.

Paul continues to teach the Galatians how they are to live the Christian life. If they have been justified by faith alone in Christ, then how should they live? In many ways the gospel seems stunningly free—God justifies us because we believe in Christ and not because of our own good works. Does this therefore mean that a person can live in whatever sinful manner he may choose? Absolutely not. Paul's famous retort to such a question should always come to mind: "By no means! How can we who died to sin still live in it?" (Rom 6:2). In the previous section, Paul told the Galatians to use their Christ-wrought, Spirit-applied freedom as an opportunity to serve and love one another. But Paul has not forgotten his theology. The Galatians

155

were not supposed to start with faith in Christ and end with their works. Rather, Paul points to the source of the Galatian fruit—their union with Christ.

Christ came in order to pour out the Holy Spirit upon the creation and to bring forth a new creation. The epicenter of this new creational activity lies within the church. The apostle Peter told the crowds at Pentecost: "Being therefore exalted at the right hand of God, and having received from the Father the promise of the Holy Spirit, he [Christ] has poured out this that you yourselves are seeing and hearing" (Acts 2:33). For this reason Paul calls Christ a "life-giving Spirit" (1 Cor. 15:45*). When Paul conveys these truths to the Galatians, he does not do so in static, timeless, abstract doctrinal propositions. Instead, he tells the Galatians they can love one another only if they "walk by the Spirit" (Gal. 5:16). Once again, Paul employs language from Israel's past—in other words, Paul's doctrine is enrobed in Israel's narrative history—the Exodus. Looking to Israel's desert wanderings is key to understanding Paul's instructions to walk by the Spirit.

Israel's Spirit-Led Desert Wanderings

Paul has employed language and images from Israel's past to characterize life under the Mosaic covenant. Before Christ came and inaugurated the new creation, Israel was "held captive" and "imprisoned" under the law (Gal. 3:23). Paul told the Galatians that, under the Mosaic covenant, they were "enslaved" by "weak and worthless elementary principles of the world" (Gal. 4:8–9). For a first-century Jew steeped in the knowledge of the Old Testament, these words and images would undoubtedly invoke Israel's slavery under Pharaoh in Egypt. By this language, Paul argues that the law was akin to Pharaoh; Christ, one greater than Moses, delivered God's people from the bondage of the law. But Israel's Exodus narrative did not end with their miraculous deliverance at the Red Sea.

Walk by the Spirit

The prophet Isaiah explains that when God led his people by Moses and "put in the midst of them his Holy Spirit who caused his glorious arm to go at the right hand of Moses, who divided the waters before them . . . who led them through the depths . . . the Spirit of the LORD gave them rest" (Isa. 63:11–14). This suggests that the cloud by day and pillar of fire by night that led Israel was in fact the Holy Spirit. The prophet Nehemiah offers important corroborating evidence. The prophet recounts how, even in the face of Israel's idolatry with the golden calf, God "did not forsake them in the wilderness" (Neh. 9:19). In what way did God maintain his presence with Israel: "The pillar of cloud to lead them in the way did not depart from them by day, nor the pillar of fire by night to light for them the way by which they should go. You gave your good Spirit to instruct them and did not withhold your manna from their mouth and gave them water for their thirst" (Neh. 9:19–20). Not only did God's Spirit lead Israel on the Exodus, but he also remained in their midst—he instructed them and saw to their every need. The psalmist reflects this very conclusion in his use of language evocative of Israel coming out of the Red Sea onto dry ground: "Teach me to do your will, for you are my God! Let your good Spirit lead me on level ground!" (Ps. 143:10) So, Israel was led by the Spirit, and therefore walked by the Spirit.[1]

Walk by the Spirit

Against the Exodus backdrop, Paul's instruction has greater depth: "But I say, walk by the Spirit, and you will not gratify the desires of the flesh" (Gal. 5:16). Paul exhorts the Galatians to continue on the path upon which they have been placed. For Old Testament Israel, the temptation was to return to the bondage of Egypt. For the Galatians, however, the temptation was

---

1. William N. Wilder, *Echoes of the Exodus Narrative in the Context and Background of Galatians 5:18* (New York: Peter Lang, 2001), 121–174.

to return to the bondage of the Mosaic covenant. Paul did not point the Galatians to themselves, to look within to find the will power to deny themselves. Instead, they were to look to Christ and seek the Holy Spirit: "For the desires of the flesh are against the Spirit, and the desires of the Spirit are against the flesh, for these are opposed to each other, to keep you from doing the things you want to do" (Gal. 5:17).

The two realms, flesh and Spirit, are completely antithetical—there is no agreement between them. They are two different ages, what Paul has called the "present evil age" (Gal. 1:4), and the new creation that has dawned in Christ; Paul elsewhere refers to the "age to come" (Eph. 1:21). Each age is marked by different conduct. The present evil age is marked by sexual immorality, impurity, sensuality, idolatry, sorcery, enmity, strife, jealousy, fits of anger, rivalries, dissensions, divisions, envy, drunkenness, orgies, and the like (Gal. 5:19–21). The age to come, the epoch that has dawned through the work of the last Adam and the outpouring of the life-giving Spirit, is marked by love, joy, peace, patience, kindness, goodness, faithfulness, gentleness, and self-control (Gal. 5:22–23).[2]

For all of these reasons, then, Paul confidently informs the Galatians: "But if you are led by the Spirit, you are not under the law" (Gal. 5:18). The Galatians were freed from the bondage of the law and from the dominion of Satan, sin, and death. They were freed and had the law of God written upon their hearts (Jer. 31:31–33). Paul wanted the Galatians to know that the power to manifest the fruit of the Spirit did not come from themselves but from Christ and the Spirit. Hence, Paul told the Galatians to breathe the air of the new creation, if you will. Were they to return to the bondage of the law, then they would breathe the sin-polluted air of the present evil age; this would have an injuri-

---

2. J. Gresham Machen, *Notes on Galatians*, ed. John H. Skilton (Philadelphia: Presbyterian and Reformed, 1972), 30–33.

ous effect on their sanctification. If they looked heavenward, to Christ seated in the heavenly places, and relied upon the Holy Spirit, then they would manifest his fruit. The air of the new creation would fill their lungs and enable them to live for Christ.

Loving Others in the Power of the Spirit

Paul's point is simple—seek the Holy Spirit in order to love. As simple as this message is, it is important to note how a person can seek Christ and the Spirit. In an age rampant with mysticism (finding God within), pantheism (finding God everywhere), and panentheism (finding God in all things), the tendency might be for people to seek Christ and the Spirit through these different routes. To stave off this temptation, Paul instructs us with his continued appeal. God did not redeem Israel from Egypt, drop them in the desert, and leave them to fend for themselves. To be sure, the Israelites falsely charged God with this type of faithlessness (Exod. 14:11–12; Num. 21:5), but when God redeemed Israel, he provided for their every need. He led them by the cloud-presence of the Spirit—when the Spirit moved, Israel was supposed to follow (Exod. 13:21; Num. 9:17; Neh. 9:12). Israel did not need a map—they simply had to walk by the Spirit. When Israel was hungry, God gave them manna to eat (Exod. 16:4–5). When they were thirsty, God gave them water to drink (Exod. 17:1–7; Num. 20: 1–13).

The fulfillment of these shadows has come with the advent of Christ. God has redeemed us out from under the bondage of the law and the dominion of Satan, sin, and death. Though we enter the age to come by faith in Christ, we still pilgrim in the wilderness, in the midst of the "present evil age" (Gal. 1:4). But like Israel of old, God provides for our every need. God feeds us with the manna from heaven, Christ:

> I am the bread of life. Your fathers ate the manna in
> the wilderness, and they died. This is the bread that

> comes down from heaven, so that one may eat of it and not die. I am the living bread that came down from heaven. If anyone eats of this bread, he will live forever. And the bread that I will give for the life of the world is my flesh. (John 6:48–51)

God quenches our thirst with living water: "Whoever drinks of the water that I will give him will never be thirsty again. The water that I will give him will become in him a spring of water welling up to eternal life" (John 4:14). The water that Christ gave is the Holy Spirit; Jesus said: "Whoever believes in me, as the Scripture has said, 'Out of his heart will flow rivers of living water'" (John 7:38). The apostle John adds the following explanatory comment: "Now this he said about the Spirit, whom those who believed in him were to receive, for as yet the Spirit had not been given, because Jesus was not yet glorified" (John 7:39). Paul is not the only one to build upon the Exodus narrative; Jesus clearly establishes a type/antitype relationship between Israel's redemption and the greater salvation that he would bring.

If all of these things are true, then we can rest assured that God has provided the sustenance that we need for our pilgrimage through the wilderness of this present evil age. We do not have to go off wandering about looking for Christ and the Spirit because Jesus has indwelled us through the Holy Spirit and given us his written Word. We can therefore find Christ in reading the Word but, especially, in the preaching of the Word. Each and every Lord's Day, ministers point to the rock that has been stricken and call people to the water that flows from it in the midst of a dry and thirsty land—they distribute the manna from heaven as they preach Christ and him crucified. If our desire, then, is to walk by the Spirit so that we would not gratify the desires of the flesh, then we must seek Christ by his appointed means—Word and sacrament. As Moses's face was aglow from being in the presence of God (Exod. 34:29–35), so too we are

Walk by the Spirit

transformed and conformed into the image of Christ as we draw near to him in worship. As the all-powerful Word goes forth—the same Word that brought worlds into existence—God feeds, provides, transforms, sanctifies, and saves His elect.

How sad that spiritual bulimia and anorexia plague the church. So many in the church engorge themselves on the Word and then as soon as they leave, vomit it out. Others simply avoid the Word altogether. Without spiritual nourishment, we are bound to return to our former bondage in our hunger and thirst. We will seek the table of the world and all it has to offer and stuff ourselves. And as the old adage goes, "You are what you eat." Alternatively, we can seek Christ and the Spirit—we can walk by the Spirit and seek him through the means of grace. God in Christ through the Spirit has set a sumptuous feast before us—our triune Lord has prepared a table for us in the midst of our enemies and invited us to sup with him.

We have been freed from the despotic powers of Satan, sin, and death, by the life, death, and resurrection of Christ. Now, Jesus Christ our Great Shepherd leads us through the wilderness on the last and final Exodus. Christ leads us by the presence of the Holy Spirit, like Israel of old being led by the cloud by day and the pillar of fire by night. In our pilgrimage to the heavenly Jerusalem, we must be led by the Holy Spirit. We are prone to wander, and, at times, we even try to return to the bondage from which we have been redeemed. Walk by the Spirit, therefore, and you will not gratify the desires of the flesh. If you are led by the Spirit, you are not under the law.

18

The Fruit of the Spirit, Part I

GALATIANS 5:19–25

But the fruit of the Spirit is love, joy, peace, patience, kindness, goodness, faithfulness, gentleness, self-control; against such things there is no law. And those who belong to Christ Jesus have crucified the flesh with its passions and desires. If we live by the Spirit, let us also walk by the Spirit.

George Santayana (1863–1952), a famous Spanish-American philosopher, once wrote, "Those who cannot remember the past are condemned to repeat it."[1] This saying certainly captures the important point that failing to learn from both the successes and failures of the past results in an unnecessary repetition of errors. Paul certainly wanted the Galatians to learn from the past—he wanted them to understand that their redemption was something that God began long ago, before they ever had the

---

1. George Santayana, *The Life of Reason or the Phases of Human Progress* (London: Archibald Constable & Co., Ltd., 1906), 284.

opportunity to offer anything to God. Paul also wanted the Galatians to remember Israel's past failures and therefore learn that their salvation ultimately did not hinge on their own fidelity, but upon God's faithfulness to his covenant promises.

In the previous section, we began to explore Paul's famous passage from Galatians on the fruit of the Spirit.[2] The apostle writes about the ongoing fulfillment of ancient Old Testament prophecies. Paul and the Galatians shared the same scriptural environment—the Old Testament—and there were certain concepts and ideas with which any devout Old Testament-reading Jew would have been familiar. We have seen some of these concepts and ideas throughout Paul's epistle, especially the frequent allusions to the Exodus. So far, Paul has employed the Exodus to characterize life under the law as one of slavery, bondage, captivity, and imprisonment, parallel to Israel's bondage in Egypt. On the other hand, Paul has characterized life in Christ, the antitype of Moses the deliverer, as one of freedom marked by the leading of the Spirit.

Just as the Holy Spirit led the Israelites through the wilderness in the cloud by day and the pillar of fire by night, so now he leads the pilgrim children of promise: "But I say, walk by the Spirit, and you will not gratify the desires of the flesh" (Gal. 5:16). What we might not realize is that Paul continues this Old Testament theme of the final exodus in the verses that follow. He begins to add layers of other Old Testament promises and prophecies, especially those promising a verdant and fruitful new creation.

Israel's Unfruitfulness

It is necessary that we back up and look at the broader storyline of redemptive history for a moment, specifically God's displeasure with Israel. Isaiah employs the prophetic parable

2. See G. K. Beale, "The Old Testament Background of Paul's Reference to 'the Fruit of the Spirit' in Galatians 5:22," *Bulletin for Biblical Research* 15/1 (2005): 1–38.

of Israel as Yahweh's vineyard. He recounts how God carefully planted his vineyard on a fertile hill, hewed out a wine vat for it, and then eagerly waited for the vineyard to yield grapes. Much to his displeasure, God's vineyard produced wild grapes. Isaiah then pulls back the prophetic veil to reveal that Israel was God's vineyard and the wild grapes that she produced were bloodshed, violence, and wickedness, instead of the righteousness and justice he expected (Isa. 5:1–7). Keep this in mind, therefore: Israel as the fruitless vineyard. Another thing to keep in mind is Paul's subtle but ongoing critique of the Judaizers: if Old Testament Israel failed in her attempts to produce righteousness by adherence to the law, then surely the Judaizers will likewise fail. Paul's overall strategy is brilliant, as he is outdoing the Judaizers in their appeal to the Old Testament!

The Coming Fruitful Servant

After Isaiah's prophecy was written, God sent his people into exile for their wickedness, but he gave assurances that he would still send his promised servant. From the vantage point of exile, however, it would appear as though God's covenant promises to his people—especially the promise of a forthcoming Davidic descendent to rule over Israel—were all but forgotten. But Isaiah gave the future exiles hope. From the stump of Jesse, the apparently cut-off lineage of David, a shoot would come forth and "bear fruit" (Isa. 11:1). That Isaiah mentions the production of fruit is key, as it stands in contrast to the wild fruit (bloodshed and violence) of faithless Israel (Isa. 5:1–7). But how would this fruit come about? The Holy Spirit would rest upon the shoot from the stump of Jesse; this Davidic descendant would rule in righteousness and faithfulness (Isa. 11:2–5). Isaiah goes on to write: "In days to come Jacob shall take root, Israel shall blossom and put forth shoots and fill the whole world with fruit"

(Isa. 27:6). Isaiah prophesies of a time when Israel would fill the entire world with fruit.

God promises through the prophet that the shoot from the stump of Jesse, Jesus Christ, will bear this fruit. The work of causing the earth to sprout with fruit, however, is not the work of the servant alone. The fruit will come from Christ and the Holy Spirit, who will be poured out on creation until "the wilderness becomes a fruitful field, and the fruitful field is deemed a forest." The language of "fruit" is symbolic for justice, righteousness, and its effect, peace (Isa. 32:14–17; cf. 44:2–4). The work of the Spirit-anointed fruit-bearing servant is coterminous with the outpouring of the Spirit, which also produces fruit: "Shower, O heavens, from above, and let the clouds rain down righteousness; let the earth open, that salvation and righteousness may bear fruit; let the earth cause them both to sprout; I the LORD have created it" (Isa. 45:8).

All of this imagery is creation-laden and echoes the opening chapters of Genesis, especially as Jesus Christ created the heavens and earth through the agency of the Holy Spirit (Col. 1:16; Gen 1:2). The creation was completed and ended with the first Adam standing in the midst of a host of fruit-bearing trees. Notice, then, how God characterizes Israel's renewal: "For the LORD comforts Zion; he comforts all her waste places and makes her wilderness like Eden, her desert like the garden of the LORD; joy and gladness will be found in her, thanksgiving and the voice of song" (Isa. 51:3). The renewal of the creation through Christ and the Spirit is likened to the pristine conditions of the garden-temple of Eden.

The Fruit of the Spirit

The first Adam was placed in the world to rule over it, to extend God's image throughout the world, and to extend the garden-temple throughout the world. Adam failed—he rebelled against God and surrendered his reign to the powers of Satan, sin, and death. The epoch or period of Adam is marked by the works of the flesh: "Now the works of the flesh are evident: sexual immorality, impurity, sensuality, idolatry, sorcery, enmity, strife, jealousy, fits of anger, rivalries, dissensions, divisions, envy, drunkenness, orgies, and things like these" (Gal. 5:19–21). All of these things arise from the sin of Adam, and all of those who are in Adam manifest these wicked works. Note how Paul characterizes our redemption by Christ, "who gave himself for our sins to deliver us from the present evil age, according to the will of our God and Father" (Gal. 1:4).

By stark contrast, notice what Christ brings. Christ suffered the curse on our behalf so that we would receive the promised Spirit through faith (Gal. 3:13–14). The long-promised outpouring of the Spirit, not only mentioned in Isaiah but also in Joel 2:28, was performed through Christ with his ascension to the right hand of the Father (Acts 2:33). For all of these reasons, Paul calls Adam a "living being" and Christ, the "last Adam" a "life-giving Spirit" (1 Cor. 15:45*). Through the outpouring of the Spirit, God's people are indwelt and enabled to produce the fruit of the Spirit: "But the fruit of the Spirit is love, joy, peace, patience, kindness, goodness, faithfulness, gentleness, self-control; against such things there is no law" (Gal. 5:22–23). Geerhardus Vos, the well-known professor of Biblical Theology, explains what Christ has accomplished and how he has applied his redemption. He first addresses what Christ has accomplished:

> He [Christ] alone of all mankind fulfilled the law in its deepest purport and widest extent. His keeping of it proceeded from that sanctuary of his inner life where he and the Father always beheld each other's face. He made it his meat and drink to do the will of God. His human nature was an altar from which the incense of perfect consecration rose ceaselessly day

and night. He submitted to the cross and endured the shame, not merely on our behalf, but first of all in order that not one jot or one tittle of the divine justice should fall to the ground. He not only hungered and thirsted but was satisfied with the travail of his soul.

Vos then addresses the benefits that Christ has secured, in our justification, sanctification, and glorification:

And now you and I can come and take of the bread and water of life freely. Through justification we are even in this life filled with the fullness of his merit, and appear to God as spotless and blameless as though sin had never touched us. Through sanctification his holy character is impressed upon our souls, so that, notwithstanding our imperfections, God takes a true delight in us, seeing that the inner man is changed from day to day after the likeness of Christ. And the full meaning of our Lord's promise we shall know in the last day, when he shall satisfy himself in us by presenting us to God perfect in body, soul and spirit. Then shall come to pass the word that is written: "They shall hunger no more, neither thirst any more." For we shall behold God's face in righteousness and be satisfied, when we awake, with his image.[3]

Quite literally, when we walk by the Spirit, the love that we show others, the joy that we know even during trials, the peace of God that we have and share with others through the gospel—in all of these things we experience and manifest the very things God promised through the prophet Isaiah over 2,500 years ago. We live out the redemption that Christ has secured. Additionally, notice two other things.

---

3. Geerhardus Vos, *Grace and Glory* (Edinburgh: Banner of Truth, [1922] 1994), 42–43.

The Fruit of the Spirit, Part I

First, Paul warns those who exhibit the works of the flesh: "I warn you, as I warned you before, that those who do such things will not inherit the kingdom of God" (Gal. 5:21). In other words, if a person does not repent of his sin and look to Christ, he remains in the kingdom of Satan, under the fallen reign of Adam. By contrast, if we look to Christ by faith, then we inherit the kingdom of God, and Christ's kingdom is marked by righteousness. Second, notice the difference between works and fruit. Why did Paul not call it the "works of the Spirit"? I think the implication is that, ultimately, it is the Spirit, as we rest in his power, who produces his fruit in us. We do not produce these characteristics of righteousness, but rather Christ through his Spirit produces them: "I have been crucified with Christ. It is no longer I who live, but Christ who lives in me. And the life I now live in the flesh I live by faith in the Son of God, who loved me and gave himself for me" (Gal. 2:20). Through their own effort, the false teachers were trying to produce the righteousness that God required.

In a stroke of brilliant exegesis, Paul has shown the false teachers that they failed to understand how God had fulfilled the requirements of the law, not through greater efforts at obedience by his people, but through his Son: "For God has done what the law, weakened by the flesh, could not do. By sending his own Son in the likeness of sinful flesh and for sin, he condemned sin in the flesh, in order that the righteous requirement of the law might be fulfilled in us, who walk not according to the flesh but according to the Spirit" (Rom. 8:3–4).

Some people have the memory of an elephant—they forget nothing. But collectively, the people of God have a short memory. We read of Israel's complaints in the wilderness and scratch our heads in amazement. How could they believe that God brought them out to the wilderness to die when he just visited the plagues upon Egypt, miraculously divided the Red Sea, and drowned Pharaoh and his army in the very waters through which they were delivered? Why would they want to go back to Egypt? Their foolishness is readily manifest. But what we may not realize is that, when we read the Exodus narratives, in many ways we are looking in a mirror. The Galatians were quick to abandon the gospel and wanted to return to the bondage of the law. As the famous hymn, "Come Thou Fount of Every Blessing," reminds us: "Prone to wander, Lord, I feel it, prone to leave the God I love." We too have a short memory. We forget all God has done for us in Christ. In Santayana's words, we fail to remember the past, which makes us prime candidates to repeat its errors.

One thing that the Old Testament background to the fruit of the Spirit should impress upon us is how our redemption has been unfolding and active long before we were even born. Our redemption stretches back to before the foundation of the world when we were chosen in Christ (Eph. 1:3–4). We were dead in our sins and trespasses and Christ poured out the Spirit upon us, effectually called us, gave us the ability to believe, and set us on the path of righteousness. Christ's work was promised literally thousands of years ago and we are evidence—what Paul elsewhere calls a letter written, not on tablets of stone but on human hearts (2 Cor. 3:3). If God has been so faithful throughout the ages, then why do we doubt him? Why are we so quick to forget his covenant faithfulness to the saints throughout the ages? Why do we question his promises?

In the face of fear, doubts, questions, and especially sin, we must flee to our faithful covenant Lord. Again, Vos beautifully summarizes the reason we should be filled with hope:

> Thanks be to God, he is a Savior who seeks the lost, who with eyes supernaturally far-sighted discerns us a long way off, and draws our interest to himself by the sweet constraint of his grace, till we are face to face with him and our soul is saved. As once,

in the incarnation, he came down from heaven to seek mankind, so he still comes down silently from heaven in the case of each sinner, and pursues his search for that individual soul, following it through all the mazes of its waywardness and the devious paths of its folly, sometimes unto the very brink of destruction, till at last his grace overtakes it and says, "I must lodge at thy house."[4]

We must rehearse God's faithfulness throughout the ages and look to all of his promises and their fulfillment. Confront your faithlessness with God's faithfulness in Christ. In the following section, we will continue to explore the fruit of the Spirit and see what specific conduct should and should not mark the Christian.

---

4. Vos, *Grace and Glory*, 52–53.

19

The Fruit of the Spirit, Part II

GALATIANS 5:19–25

But the fruit of the Spirit is love, joy, peace, patience, kindness, goodness, faithfulness, gentleness, self-control; against such things there is no law. And those who belong to Christ Jesus have crucified the flesh with its passions and desires. If we live by the Spirit, let us also walk by the Spirit.

All too often, when people come to Paul's famous passage of the fruit of the Spirit, they treat it as if Paul has given a new law: "Thou shalt love, thou shalt be joyful, and thou shalt have peace." In technical terms, people conflate the indicatives of Scripture with its imperatives. Indicatives present a state of affairs whereas imperatives give commands. As we explore the fruit of the Spirit, we must not forget all of the indicatives that Paul has given thus far. The Galatians received by faith alone the outpouring of the Spirit through the work of Christ. Their union with Christ is the indicative. On the basis of the indicative, union with Christ, Paul could then give the Galatians imperatives such as, "You shall love your neighbor as yourself" (Gal. 5:14; Lev. 19:18). Geerhardus Vos explains the danger of conflating the indicatives and the imperatives:

> There are still abroad forms of a Christless gospel. There prevails still a subtle form of legalism which would rob the Savior of his crown and glory, earned by the cross, and would make of him a second Moses, offering us the stones of the law instead of the life-bread of the gospel. And, oh the pity and shame of it, the Jesus that is being preached but too often is a Christ after the flesh, a religious genius, the product of evolution, powerless to save! Let us pray that it may be given to the church to repudiate and cast out this error with the resoluteness of Paul.[1]

We cannot reverse the order—we cannot make imperatives the means by which we obtain the indicatives. In other words, we cannot submit our obedience to God's law as the means by which we secure our union with Christ. Rather, our union with Christ enables us to obey the moral imperatives of Scripture. As one seventeenth-century Particular Baptist theologian, Benjamin Keach (1640–1704), has put it: "You must first have union with him, before you can bring forth fruit to God; you must act *from* life, and not *for* life."[2]

So as Paul sets forth the fruit of the Spirit, we should distinguish the indicatives and imperatives. The Spirit produces his holy fruit within us. We cannot pull ourselves up by our moral bootstraps in the effort to love, to have joy, or to produce peace within our hearts. Throughout this examination, Paul's words should echo in our hearts and minds: "I have been crucified

---

1. Geerhardus Vos, *Grace and Glory* (Edinburgh: Banner of Truth, [1922] 1994), 102.

2. Benjamin Keach, *The Marrow of True Justification Without Works* (London: n.p., 1692), 37. Emphasis added.

with Christ. It is no longer I who live, but Christ who lives in me. And the life I now live in the flesh I live by faith in the Son of God, who loved me and gave himself for me" (Gal. 2:20). In this vein, if Christ indwells us through the Spirit, then we should realize that we cannot abstract the fruit from him. Paul does not point to abstractions about love, let alone define it in a worldly manner. Rather, *Christ* defines the fruit of the Spirit. Therefore, in our quest to understand the fruit of the Spirit, our lodestar can be no one else but Christ.

Love, Joy, Peace

The greatest manifestation of love the world has ever seen is Christ's love for fallen sinners. As Jesus told his disciples: "Greater love has no one than this, that someone lay down his life for his friends" (John 15:13). But what makes Christ's love jaw-dropping is that he loved us even while we hated him. This is perfect love (Matt. 5:43–48). Love, then, is not simply an emotion—a warm feeling that we might have for another. It is not an ill-defined mantra, like the Beatles' song, "All You Need Is Love," where the virtue is extolled as "all you need" and the enabling comes from realizing that "there's nothing you can make that can't be made" or "nothing you can know that isn't known." Love is concrete action on another's behalf even in the face of hostility and hatred.

Paul's famous chapter on love confirms this: love is patient, kind, never envies or boasts, is not arrogant or rude, never insists on its own way, is not irritable, resentful, and rejoices with the truth (1 Cor. 13:4–7). All of these things characterize Christ and must therefore characterize Christians. As Martin Luther once observed, Christians are certainly not justified by their works "since they already are righteous through faith, but that in the liberty of the Spirit they shall by so doing serve others and the authorities themselves and obey their will freely and out of love."[3] A Christ-shaped love is the antithesis to the world's perversion of it—sexual immorality and orgies (expressions of love without boundaries), idolatry (the love of something else other than God), enmity (hateful actions towards others made in the image of God), and jealousy (lusting after something God has seen fit not to give us). All too often, the perversions of true love have infected the church. One of the most common forms of this is the prevalence of pornography.

Joy is not necessarily always a feeling of exuberance. The Scriptures wed joy and suffering in Christ's ministry: "Jesus, the founder and perfecter of our faith, who for the joy that was set before him endured the cross, despising the shame, and is seated at the right hand of the throne of God" (Heb. 12:2). If we believe that joy is something we generate ourselves, then perhaps we might lack joy during times of suffering. But if we recognize that it is a fruit of the Spirit, then as Paul writes, we will be able to "rejoice always" (1 Thess. 5:16). The Spirit produces in us great joy when we seek the Father's will in all things. We can be filled with joy knowing that God forms Christ in us and that we bring glory to him through life's trials. As a mother in the throes of a painful childbirth has great joy in knowing that her child will be born, so too, in all circumstances, Christians are filled with joy when they walk by the Spirit. A Puritan prayer captures a heart that is gripped by the joy of the Spirit:

> For my joy thou hast sent the Comforter,
> multiplied thy promises,
> shown me my future happiness,
> given me a living fountain.
> Thou art preparing joy for me and me for joy;
> I pray for joy, wait for joy, long for joy;
> give me more than I can hold, desire, or think of.

---

3. Martin Luther, *The Freedom of a Christian*, in *Martin Luther's Basic Theological Writings*, ed. Timothy F. Lull (Minneapolis, MN: Fortress, [1520] 1989), 621.

The Fruit of the Spirit, Part II

> Measure out to me my times and degrees of joy
> at my work, business, duties.
> If I weep at night, give me joy in the morning.
> Let me rest in the thought of thy love,
> pardon for sin, my title to heaven,
> my future unspotted state.[4]

Joy is not the absence of pain or suffering but rather a contentment grounded in Christ and steadfast in the knowledge that one is firmly in the Savior's grasp.

Joy is often attended by peace (Rom. 14:17; 15:13). Before our redemption, our biggest problem is that we are at enmity with God—we hate him (Rom. 3:10–18; Eph. 2:1–3). But Christ is our great peacemaker: "Therefore, since we have been justified by faith, we have peace with God through our Lord Jesus Christ" (Rom. 5:1). If we have peace with God through Christ, then this God-given peace should permeate the rest of our lives—we should, insofar as it depends on us, be at peace with all people, but especially with those in the church. Christ broke down the dividing wall of hostility between Jew and Gentile (Eph. 2:15–16). Christ *is* the church's peace. This was the very thing that the false teachers were jeopardizing—they were rebuilding the wall of division by their insistence on circumcision. They were creating strife, rivalries, dissensions, and divisions— the very opposite of peace. However, if the church is united to Christ, then it should be marked by peace.

Beyond the corporate peace that should be found in the church, the lives of individual Christians should also be marked by peace. When the Holy Spirit produces peace within us, all hell might break loose around us, but we will not be shaken. The famous hymn, "It is Well With My Soul," captures the nature of Christian peace. The author, Horatio G. Spafford, had

---

4. "Joy," in *The Valley of Vision*, ed. Arthur Bennett (Edinburgh: Banner of Truth, [1975] 2007), 292.

suffered a series of traumatic losses—his young son died and he soon thereafter lost his wealth in the Great Chicago Fire. He then sought to travel to Europe with his family but was unable to go with them. Tragically, the boat sank and Spafford lost his four daughters—his wife alone was spared. Yet, in the midst of such tumult, he could still write: "When peace, like a river attendeth my way,/ when sorrows like sea billows roll;/ whatever my lot, thou hast taught me to say,/ 'It is well, it is well with my soul.'" Only one indwelled by the Spirit of God can have the strength to write these words in the face of such loss. Note how Paul combines joy and peace even in the face of trials:

> Rejoice in the Lord always; again I will say, Rejoice. Let your reasonableness be known to everyone. The Lord is at hand; do not be anxious about anything, but in everything by prayer and supplication with thanksgiving let your requests be made known to God. And the peace of God, which surpasses all understanding, will guard your hearts and your minds in Christ Jesus. (Philippians 4:4–7)

Patience, Kindness, Goodness

Mention the word patience and Job likely comes to mind. Job's patience is legendary, as he sat atop a pile of rubble awaiting an answer from the Lord for his many questions. But we should recognize that Job prefigures Christ—the man who suffered, not for his sin, but because of his righteousness. Christ patiently dealt with his, at times dimwitted, disciples when they frequently misunderstood his teaching. Christ patiently dealt with the crowds who constantly pressed in on him looking for food, healing, and miracles. Christ patiently dealt even with the religious leaders in spite of their hatred, wicked scheming, and obstreperous arguments. Christ produces this same patience, through the Holy Spirit, in his people. When the world might respond in a fit of anger because things do not immediately go as expected or desired, God's people manifest patience even in the face of annoying or difficult circumstances.

Indeed, Christ's patience towards his bride even in the face of her faithlessness is also a manifestation of kindness. When someone deserves punishment, but receives pardon, this is an act of kindness. Paul calls our redemption that we receive in Christ "the goodness and loving kindness of God" (Titus 3:4). That Paul combines goodness and kindness should also tell us that the two virtues are closely related. If we have been the recipients of the kindness and goodness of God, then how can we fail to show the same to others around us? If we hated God but nevertheless received his kindness and goodness in Christ, should we not do likewise to those who hate us? The present evil age is marked by the darkness of fits of anger; hence, those who are united to Christ have the opportunity to shine the light of goodness and kindness into this sin-darkened world. Rather than seeking revenge or responding with sarcasm or anger, our desire should be to respond with kindness and goodness.

Faithfulness, Gentleness, Self-control

God has certainly been faithful to his covenant promises throughout the ages. In this respect, Paul writes: "For all the promises of God in him are yea, and in him Amen, unto the glory of God by us" (2 Cor. 1:20 KJV). In other words, Christ is the fulfillment of God's promises—he manifests the faithfulness of the triune Lord. If faithfulness marks our covenant Lord, then it should also mark His people since we are being renewed in the image of Christ. In a world marked by divisions, dissensions, and jealousy, God's children should be marked by loyalty and dependability. All too often, however, God's people are marked by faithlessness. Husbands and wives vow to be faithful to one another and then break those vows. Husbands, for example, may not go out and engage a prostitute, but the scores of pornographic images on their computers betray their infidelity. At many times, Christians are faithless in their work-ethic and no different than the unbelieving world. They are late to work, leave work early, pilfer company property, or use company resources for personal gain. To say the least, this type of conduct should never mark God's people. We should be a people faithful to the Lord and faithful to our word. Our loyal-ties must begin and end with Christ.

Gentleness and self-control, though different virtues, are closely related. The world around us is often devoid of these vir-tues. People tend to lack the self-control to guard their tongues, so they lash out with harsh and cruel words. As the recipients of God's grace in Christ, we should be the gentlest of all people. God does not immediately give us the just deserts for our sins; when sinned against, should we not respond gently? Should we not respond with self-control? This is something that Paul will later exhort the Galatians to exercise—gentleness towards a brother who has given offense to the church (Gal. 6:1).

As we meditate upon the fruit of the Spirit, we must re-member two things. First, we are incapable of effecting our own moral and spiritual transformation. We cannot save ourselves. Only Christ saves us. Hence, Paul writes: "And those who be-long to Christ Jesus have crucified the flesh with its passions and desires" (Gal. 5:24). The only way we will subdue our sin-ful passions—our sexual immorality, idolatry, anger, drunken-ness, and the like—is if Christ redeems us from the dominion of Satan, sin, and death. Like Israel leaving the furnace of Egypt behind, Christ liberates us from the tyranny of Satan, sin, and death and the bondage of the law. Christ puts to death our sin-ful nature with its passions and desires. Once freed, we must seek the power of the Holy Spirit so that he continues to pro-

The Fruit of the Spirit, Part II

duce these fruits in us: "If we live by the Spirit, let us also walk
by the Spirit" (Gal. 5:25).

Part of the reason why many Christians struggle to manifest the fruit of the Spirit is that they are unwilling to look
into the mirror of the law so they can identify their sin. Or
perhaps, having looked at the law, they find their sin, but are
unwilling to repent of it, turn from it, seek Christ, and walk
in the Spirit. Vos explains the nature of true repentance:

> True repentance strips sin of all that is accidental. It
> resembles an inner chamber where no one and noth-
> ing else is admitted except God and the sinner and
> his sin. Into that chamber all the great penitents like
> David and Paul and Augustine and Luther have en-
> tered, and each one in the bitter anguish of his soul
> has borrowed the words of the psalmist: "Against
> thee, thee only have I sinned, and done this evil in
> thy sight, that thou mightest be justified when thou
> speakest, and be clear when thou judgest." A repen-
> tant sinner acquits God and condemns himself. And
> for the very reason that his consciousness of sin is
> God-centered, he is also alive to his inward serious-
> ness. He learns to trace it in the recesses and abysses
> of his inmost life, where even the eye of self-scrutiny
> would otherwise scarcely penetrate, but in which
> the eyes of God are at home, where all our iniquities
> stand naked before him and our secret sins in the
> light of his countenance. If it is characteristic of sin
> to excuse itself, it is no less characteristic of repen-
> tance to scorn all subterfuge and to judge of itself, as
> it were, with the very veracity of God.[5]

If you regularly fail to manifest the fruit of the Spirit, perhaps
part of the answer to your wrestling with God lies in the absence of repentance. Look at yourself in the mirror of the law
and ask Christ through the Word and Spirit to convict you of

5. Vos, *Grace and Glory*, 37–38.

your sin that you might turn from it, flee to him, and walk by the Spirit. Our desires, prayers, and actions should reflect the idea that we are to be marked by fruit of the Spirit and not the works of the flesh. Pray that you will be so marked—that you might edify the body of Christ and bring glory to our triune Lord.

20

Bearing One Another's Burdens

GALATIANS 5:26–6:5

Bear one another's burdens, and so fulfill the law of Christ. For if anyone thinks he is something, when he is nothing, he deceives himself. But let each one test his own work, and then his reason to boast will be in himself alone and not in his neighbor. For each will have to bear his own load.

What does the fruit of the Spirit look like as it is applied to the Christian life? This is a question that Paul would likely have faced and is, in a manner of speaking, the question that Paul answers in this section. But first remember, that the fruit of the Spirit comes as the result of the work of Christ. Second, the benefits of Christ's redemption can be accessed only by grace alone through faith alone in Christ alone. Third, we do not produce this fruit, but rather the Holy Spirit produces it. In other words, Christ is not a new Moses who has given us a new law to perform so that we can somehow earn God's favor by our obedience. Instead, our justification yields the fruit of our sanctification. Or, our right standing with God that comes by faith alone, worked in us by the Holy Spirit, also brings his transformative work in our lives. As Machen has explained: "This forensic aspect of salvation is intimately connected with the 'vital' aspect; the new and right relation to God as Judge always goes together with the new life which the sinner possesses after he has been made a new creature by the Spirit of God."[1] In Paul's language, we must seek to ensure our faith works through love (Gal. 5:6). Christians are not idle in matters pertaining to their sanctification. Instead, we exert great effort in pursuing Christ and manifesting his holiness in word, thought, and deed.

Marked by Humility

Paul begins by exhorting the Galatians: "Let us not become conceited, provoking one another, envying one another" (Gal. 5:26). Spirit-indwelt saints are supposed to exercise Christ-formed conduct towards others in the church. We are to be void of conceit, pride, and arrogance. We are not to provoke one another, that is, purposely to incite anger in another person. The church is also supposed to be a place that is not marked by envy, a work of the flesh (Gal. 5:21), whether the envy of respect, influence, possessions, or place in life.

We can contrast the fallen kingdom of Adam with the church. In particular, even in the pre-fallen state, what was it that caused Adam to sin, reach out, and try to grasp equality with God by eating from the forbidden tree (cf. Phil. 2:5–11)? It was undoubtedly conceit and arrogance, as he thought more highly of his own desires than he did the desires of God. It was also undoubtedly his envy. The Serpent told the man and the woman that they would become like God if they ate of the fruit,

---

1. J. Gresham Machen, *Notes on Galatians*, ed. John H. Skilton (Philadelphia: Presbyterian and Reformed, 1972), 160.

and rather than be content with the position and state that God had given them, they instead envied what they did not have. By contrast, the new creation brought about by the work of Christ and the outpouring of the Holy Spirit is not supposed to be marked by such conduct. It is to be marked by humility before the Lord and one another and by contentment with where the Lord has placed us.

Paul also explains one of the ways in which gentleness manifests itself in the day-to-day life of the church: "Brothers, if anyone is caught in any transgression, you who are spiritual should restore him in a spirit of gentleness. Keep watch on yourself, lest you too be tempted" (Gal. 6:1). Paul characterizes those who are marked by gentleness as those who are "spiritual." By "spiritual," Paul does not mean those who float around on a cloud of piety, but rather those who are indwelt by the Holy Spirit—those who have entered the new creation. Those who are spiritual, then, are supposed to be willing to restore, with gentleness, anyone who is caught in any transgression, any sin. Such gentleness is undoubtedly rooted in the knowledge of the gentleness that the Lord has shown to all sinners who have been united to Christ.

No one can stand in the place of God and, with a perfect righteousness, preside in judgment over another. Rather, all of us stand in God's presence as forgiven sinners and, therefore, when it comes to restoring a repentant sinner, we should do so in gentleness and love, avoiding grudge-holding and bitterness. Moreover, the spiritual person does this because he knows that he too can fall into the same sin. The moment we think we are beyond or above certain sins, we expose ourselves to greater temptation. The one who thinks he is above the sin of adultery, for example, is likely closer to falling into unfaithfulness than the one who has a healthy fear concerning his own weakness.

Evangelical Obedience

Paul summarizes the way that those who are spiritual are supposed to treat one another: "Bear one another's burdens, and so fulfill the law of Christ" (Gal. 6:2). When Paul writes of the "law of Christ," he does not establish Jesus as a new lawgiver in opposition to Moses (i.e., the law of Christ versus the law of Moses). Recall that Paul wrote: "The whole law is fulfilled in one word: 'You shall love your neighbor as yourself'" (Gal. 5:14). Because of Christ's fulfillment of the demands of the law, believers are enabled and equipped to fulfill the law and love their neighbor (Rom. 8:3–4). Older commentators such as William Perkins helpfully distinguish between *legal* and *evangelical* obedience. Perkins writes:

> There are two kinds of fulfilling the law: one *legal*, and the other *evangelical. Legal* is, when men do all things required in the law, and that by themselves and in themselves. Thus none ever fulfilled the law, but Christ, and Adam before his fall. The *evangelical* manner of fulfilling the law, is to believe in Christ, who fulfilled the law for us: and withal to endeavor in the whole man, to obey God in all his precepts.[2]

For the believer, the new component is not the law per se but the source of his obedience, namely his union with Christ.[3] Notice how Paul describes gently restoring the repentant sinner—bearing one another's burdens. The restoration of a repentant sinner requires a mindset that is contrary to what we often find in the church. So often, we distance ourselves from the sin of another. People, for example, will mentally distance

---

2. William Perkins, *A Commentary on Galatians*, ed. Gerald T. Shepherd (New York: Pilgrim Press, [1617] 1989), 165.

3. Herman Ridderbos, *Galatians*, NICNT (Grand Rapids, MI: Eerdmans, 1972), 213.

themselves and say in their hearts, "Oh, I would never do such a thing." In this way, we alienate the one who has sinned. Instead, Paul defines restoring the sinner as *bearing his burden*, an act which requires proximity.

Ideally, when a church confronts a sinner with his sin, the whole process should be marked by corporate humility. The church should corporately examine itself and repent of its own sin; she should also pray on behalf of the person guilty of great sin. She should pray that he would repent and be restored to full fellowship within the church. So often this is not at all the case—those who are caught in public sin are ostracized under the pretense of piety. To do this, I believe, is to think too much of ourselves and too little of the work of Christ and the Spirit in our lives.

This is why Paul writes: "For if anyone thinks he is something, when he is nothing, he deceives himself" (Gal. 6:3). To borrow an apt illustration, we forget that we are beggars who have graciously been given a sumptuous meal. When other beggars come looking for food, we act as if we purchased, cooked, and provided the meal for ourselves and therefore look down upon the other beggars. But if we constantly remind ourselves that Christ and the Holy Spirit have mercifully provided the meal, then we will be less prone to esteem ourselves so highly. Or to put it in Pauline terms, we will be led by the Spirit and not try to live in the fallen kingdom of Adam, the one from which we have been redeemed. Paul elaborates upon this idea in verse 4, which at first glance seems a bit odd: "But let each one test his own work, and then his reason to boast will be in himself alone and not in his neighbor" (Gal. 6:4). This sentence seems a bit confusing if not outright contrary to everything that Paul has written thus far. How can Paul say that a person could find reason to boast in himself alone? Are we not to boast only in Christ?

First, Paul tells the Galatians to test their own works. This means, I believe, that if we test our obedience by holding it up to the demands of the law and against the perfect righteousness of Christ, we will always find our obedience wanting. We cannot meet the demands of the law and even our best works are tainted with sin. Second, when people boast in themselves they often do so with an eye not to Christ, but to man. In this particular case, the false teachers at Galatia were boasting about the success of their work in others. They were boasting that they had convinced many Gentiles to accept circumcision, and therefore were boasting in their neighbors. I think we can confirm this conclusion from what Paul says toward the end of chapter six: "For even those who are circumcised do not themselves keep the law, but they desire to have you circumcised that they may boast in your flesh. But far be it from me to boast except in the cross of our Lord Jesus Christ, by which the world has been crucified to me, and I to the world" (Gal. 6:13–14).

Rather than boasting in ourselves or what we have accomplished, we should boast only in what Christ has done, and, in this particular case, Paul is saying that we should boast in what Christ has done in us. Related to this practice that Paul discourages is the idea of comparing ourselves to our fellow Christian rather than to Christ. Instead of comparing ourselves to the law and to Christ's fulfillment of it, we compare ourselves to our sinful neighbor. We think, "Well, I'm not as bad as that guy, so I'm doing fine!" To do this is to seek our sanctification, and even our salvation, in our own imperfect obedience and righteousness rather than in Christ alone.

Paul therefore writes: "For each will have to bear his own load" (Gal. 6:5). When Paul writes this, he conveys the idea that, when we stand in the presence of God, we do so alone. We cannot point to others and say, "Look how much better I am than those people over there." God evaluates us individually. We can either look to Christ by faith and receive his righteousness and perfect obedience, or we can try to stand on our own. However, if we lean on our own devices, there will be no one else to blame when we fall. We will have to give an account for every one of our actions. There will not be any justification by guilt, by poor parents, by weakness, or any other excuse we may try to conjure up.

Concern for the Church

We need constant reminders of our sinfulness, of God's grace in Christ, and our need of the Holy Spirit. Like Israel who quickly wandered from the Lord when things were going well, we too wander from him and forget how much we need God's grace in Christ. We begin to think that we somehow have arrived where we are by hard work and our own elbow grease. Such a mind-set should not characterize one who dwells in the kingdom of Christ, who has been redeemed from Satan, sin, and death, and who is now a new creature indwelt by the Holy Spirit.

Paul characterizes Christians as those who manifest the fruit of the Spirit. They are humble and content. They are burdened for the repentant sinner and desire to restore him gently. Christians do not look to others or to themselves but to Christ alone for their salvation. How much are we burdened by one another's sins? How much do we pray for one another? What about those under church discipline—how do we react to them? Do we talk to them, encourage them, and tell them how we are burdened for their repentance? Have we examined our own hearts, confessed our own similar sins to the Lord, thanked him for his grace, asked him to protect us from falling into such sins, and then fervently interceded on behalf of those under church discipline? In the light of Paul's instruction, we must seek to live in such a manner.

But Paul's instructions for the restoration of a repentant sinner do not apply simply to church members in general, but especially to the elders of a church. David Dickson, a seven-teenth-century Scottish Reformer, explains:

> He [Paul] speaks especially to the presbyters, on whom it lies by duty to recall those again to repentance who are fallen into scandals, by ecclesiastical censures, and to restore again the disjointed members of the church into their place. He commands those to use meekness toward them who through infirmity are fallen back, and not to deal severely with them, which without doubt belongs to those who have the power of punishing sinners.[4]

This can be difficult for elders because, unlike other members of the church, they are usually the ones who have to deal directly with matters of discipline. Elders often see people at their worst, when they are neck-deep in wickedness and covered in the foul stench of their sin. Elders often bear the brunt of a wayward sinner's hatred and anger. In all of these things, elders should pray that they would be filled with the love of Christ, and as our Savior cried out to our heavenly Father to forgive the people who mocked him as he hung on the cross, so too elders of the church must be prepared to bear their cross, turn the other cheek, and restore the repentant sinner with gentleness and love.

Above all else, we must recognize that as the church, as the community that is indwelled by the Holy Spirit, we must manifest the fruit of the Spirit. To manifest this fruit, however, is not something that is done in the abstract. There are concrete points in our lives where God calls us to manifest this fruit! Therefore cry out to the Lord that he would by his Spirit produce in us humility, love, and passion for him. Cry out to the Lord that he would by his Spirit place within us the desire to be

---

4. Gerald L. Bray, ed., *Galatians, Ephesians*, vol. 10, *Reformation Commentary on Scripture, New Testament* (Downers Grove, IL: InterVarsity Press, 2011), 206.

burdened for one another so that we would lift one another up in prayer and point one another to Christ. For Christ has not redeemed us so that we could continue in our former ways. No, we have crucified the flesh with its passions and desires. Therefore, let us joyfully live and walk by the Spirit.

21

Especially to the Household of Faith

GALATIANS 6:6–10

And let us not grow weary of doing good, for in due season we will reap, if we do not give up. So then, as we have opportunity, let us do good to everyone, and especially to those who are of the household of faith.

We are familiar with love, joy, peace, patience, kindness, gentleness, goodness, faithfulness, and self-control. What we might not know is how we should manifest these fruits in real-life situations. In the first portion of chapter 6, Paul elaborated on how the Galatian churches should manifest such fruits as love, patience, kindness, and gentleness in the restoration of a repentant sinner. Paul wrote: "Brothers, if anyone is caught in any transgression, you who are spiritual should restore him in a spirit of gentleness. Keep watch on yourself, lest you too be tempted" (Gal. 6:1). In other words, those who are spiritual were to manifest the fruit of the Spirit in the concrete action of gently restoring a repentant sinner.

One who is spiritual recognizes the kindness, love, and mercy that God constantly shows to him, and he therefore generously shows it to others. One who is spiritual recognizes his ability to fall into the same sins that ensnare his neighbors, so he does not deal harshly with others. One who is spiritual searches his own heart to see where he might be guilty of the same sins, and he confesses and repents of them. In the demonstration of such kindness and love, the spiritual person recognizes that he is not the source of his salvation, but that it comes from Christ and was graciously applied by the Holy Spirit. In other words, the church should be marked by, of all things, humility before the Lord and towards one another.

In the passage before us, Paul continues to show how the fruit of the Spirit should be manifest in the life of the church. In particular, Paul addresses the specific subjects of financially supporting the work of pastors, as well as showing kindness to our neighbors, but especially to the household of faith, the Church.

The Fruit of the Spirit in the Church

To understand what Paul writes in verse 6, we must first briefly note the previous verse: "For each will have to bear his own load" (Gal. 6:5). This was Paul's instruction concerning the idea that all of us will have to stand individually before the presence of God to account for our lives. We will not be able to hide behind excuses or compare ourselves to others. We can either stand alone, or we can look to Christ by faith and be covered by his righteousness. There are no other options.

Paul did not want his instruction to be misconstrued to mean that ministers, or pastors, should therefore have to provide for their own financial support. Paul therefore qualifies what he has said in verse 5 with his statement in verse 6: "One who is taught the word must share all good things with the one who teaches" (Gal. 6:6). The recipient of the teaching and preaching of the Word should share all good things with the teacher and preacher. While "all good things" is not restricted to financial support alone, it should nevertheless include it. Elsewhere, Paul explains the importance of supporting ministers in their labor of Word and sacrament: "Let the elders who rule well be considered worthy of double honor, especially those who labor in preaching and teaching. For the Scripture says, 'You shall not muzzle an ox when it treads out the grain,' and, 'The laborer deserves his wages'" (1 Tim. 5:17–18).

The fruit of the Spirit manifests itself concretely in the life of the church. So often, people do not equate spirituality with something as seemingly mundane and ordinary as seeing that the pastor receives adequate remuneration. I think the stingy mindset that plagues much of the church is often manifested when Christians go out to eat. Some Christians I know who were once servers at restaurants have observed that Christian customers would often leave a meager tip or no tip at all, or worse yet, a Bible tract instead of a tip! Leaving a Bible tract is not wrong—we should look for every opportunity to give witness to the gospel. But leaving a Bible tract *in the place of a tip* is the problem. We should not use the gospel as an excuse for our stinginess. The same attitude evidences itself in the assumption that ministers should be willing to work "for the Lord," that is, with little or no pay. Even in my short ministry, I witnessed a significant rift develop in a congregation because certain individuals did not think a prospective pastor should make more than they did. This miserly manner should never characterize a church.

Instead, a church that is marked by the Holy Spirit and his fruit will show love, kindness, and goodness to their pastor by seeing that he is well-paid. Notice how Paul characterizes seeing to the financial needs of the pastor: "Do not be deceived: God is not mocked, for whatever one sows, that will he also reap. For the one who sows to his own flesh will from the flesh reap corruption, but the one who sows to the Spirit will from the Spirit reap eternal life" (Gal. 6:7–8). That we are still in the realm of discussing the fruit of the Spirit is evident by Paul's language here.

These verses do not apply only to the way a congregation treats and supports its pastor, which would not be restricted to finances alone, but they also address the way a congregation should treat a repentant sinner. The basic idea is, you reap what you sow. In this case, if you sow works of the flesh, Paul says you will reap corruption—impurity, licentiousness, idolatry, enmity, strife, jealousy, anger, selfishness, dissension, divisions, and in the end, judgment. By contrast, the one who sows to the Spirit will reap eternal life.

Paul does not contradict what he has written before concerning justification by faith alone. Paul does not advocate a quid pro quo of good works for salvation. Rather, if you sow the fruit of the Spirit, you will reap the benefits of the Spirit. Or, I think verses 7–8 are another way of restating what Paul has previously written: "I warn you, as I warned you before, that those who do such things will not inherit the kingdom of God" (Gal. 5:21). So then, we should not lose sight of the context of Paul's instruction. Paul still writes of the fruit of the Spirit and tells his readers that they can live in only one of two worlds—the fallen kingdom of Adam, now ruled by Satan, or the eternal kingdom of Jesus Christ, the last Adam. If we are united to Christ and indwelt by the Holy Spirit, then the fruit of the Spirit should be manifest in our lives, both corporately and individually.

Here, though, Paul has given the specific examples of restoring the repentant sinner and the way a congregation treats its pastor. But Paul is not yet finished with his counsel: "And let us not grow weary of doing good, for in due season we will reap, if we do not give up" (Gal. 6:9). Sometimes Christians can grow weary as they seek to manifest the fruit of the Spirit. They demonstrate love and kindness to others, but nothing good seems to result. Paul reminds his readers that, nevertheless, the time will come to reap the harvest of the Spirit: "For I consider that the sufferings of this present time are not worth comparing with the glory that is to be revealed to us. For the creation waits with eager longing for the revealing of the sons of God" (Rom. 8:18–19). Similarly, the apostle John writes: "Beloved, we are God's children now, and what we will be has not yet appeared; but we know that when he appears we shall be like him, because we shall see him as he is" (1 John 3:2). So, in this way, in eager anticipation of the conclusion of all things, the imminent return of Christ, Paul exhorts us to continue steadfastly in sowing righteousness.

Remember the greater Old Testament backdrop of Paul's instruction concerning the fruit of the Spirit: "In days to come Jacob shall take root, Israel shall blossom and put forth shoots and fill the whole world with fruit" (Isa. 27:6). So then, we must be unflagging in our pursuit of holiness and the fruit of the Spirit. But our pursuit of the fruit is not for our own sake; the fruit the Spirit produces in us is to benefit *others*. Thus, Paul closes out this portion of chapter 6: "So then, as we have opportunity, let us do good to everyone, and especially to those who are of the household of faith" (Gal. 6:10). Notice how Paul focused initially upon the congregation's treatment of their pastor, but this love expands to the entire congregation and then beyond.

Those who are spiritual are supposed to "do good to every-one." In other words, show love, kindness, patience, gentleness, and the like to everyone we encounter. Though Paul does not state it here, we should recall Christ's teaching:

> You have heard that it was said, "You shall love your neighbor and hate your enemy." But I say to you, Love your enemies and pray for those who perse-cute you, so that you may be sons of your Father who is in heaven. For he makes his sun rise on the evil and on the good, and sends rain on the just and on the unjust. For if you love those who love you, what reward do you have? Do not even the tax collectors do the same? And if you greet only your brothers, what more are you doing than others? Do not even the Gentiles do the same? You therefore must be perfect, as your heavenly Father is perfect. (Matthew 5:43–48)

We should also note that when we hear the term *neighbor*, we should not restrict it to those who live in the immediate vicin-ity of our homes. Neither should we restrict it to people in the church. Martin Luther wonderfully summarizes how a justified Christian manifests the love of Christ in his life:

> When I have this righteousness within me, I descend from heaven like the rain that makes the earth fertile. That is, I come forth into another kingdom, and I perform good works whenever the opportunity aris-es. If I am a minister of the Word, I preach, I com-fort the saddened, I administer the sacraments. If I am a father, I rule my household and family, I train my children in piety and honesty. If I am a magis-trate, I perform the office I have received by divine command. If I am a servant, I faithfully tend to my master's affairs. In short, whoever knows for sure that Christ is his righteousness not only cheerfully and gladly works in his calling but also submits him-

self for the sake of love to magistrates, also to their wicked laws, and to everything else in this present life—even, if need be, to burden and danger. For he knows that God wants this and that his obedience pleases him.[1]

It matters not where the people come from; ours is a simple task—love everyone. We manifest the righteousness of the new creation in the midst of the darkness of the present evil age. These good works are not ostentatious or flashy but are everyday and ordinary, even though in reality they are glorious beams of light from the heavenly throne of Christ.

Paul adds a qualification to our indiscriminant love for all people, in that we are especially to show love and kindness to the household of faith, the church. That Paul uses the term "household" (*oikiakos*) is significant, in that it was an Old Testament term that was used to denote an entire family. Recall, for example, that Abraham was supposed to circumcise all of the males in his household (Gen. 17:13). When a family celebrated the Passover, they were to have one Passover lamb per household (Exod. 12:3). In the New Testament, the Scriptures speak of the church as the household of God: "So then you are no longer strangers and aliens, but you are fellow citizens with the saints and members of the household of God" (Eph. 2:19). Christ is the head of the household of God. And Christ concretely shows his love by his provident care for his household and also *through* his people to the world.

If Christ is the head of the church and we are his body, then we are the arms and hands by which Christ dispenses his love, kindness, and mercy to the rest of the church. So, when we love all people, we should do so especially with an eye to the church, the household of faith. Moreover, when we show the love of

---

1. Martin Luther, *Galatians*, vol. 26, *Luther's Works*, ed. Jaroslav Pelikan (St. Louis: Concordia, 1963), 11–12.

Christ to the household of faith, we do so ultimately to Christ himself. Recall Christ's words to this effect:

> "For I was hungry and you gave me no food, I was thirsty and you gave me no drink, I was a stranger and you did not welcome me, naked and you did not clothe me, sick and in prison and you did not visit me." Then they also will answer, saying, "Lord, when did we see you hungry or thirsty or a stranger or naked or sick or in prison, and did not minister to you?" Then he will answer them, saying, "Truly, I say to you, as you did not do it to one of the least of these, you did not do it to me." (Matthew 25:42–45)

In this sense, then, I believe it is entirely legitimate and appropriate to say that while we love all people, there are a series of concentric circles of responsibility that begin with our families first, then the church, and then the world. Each of these spheres of existence are the places where we are called to manifest the fruit of the Spirit.

Congregations, therefore, should consider how they should "do good to everyone," as Paul instructs the Galatians. But they should also remember that whatever good they do should go first and foremost to the "household of faith," the church. For example, churches should have diaconal funds to assist people who have physical or financial needs. But the lion's share of those funds should be directed to and for church members. A portion of the funds, however, should be directed to those outside the church. The same can be said regarding the amount of time that a church might invest in helping others. If a storm blows through town and wreaks havoc, the church should ensure that its members are taken care of first—the church should ensure that members have housing, food, and the like; then, they should look to care for the needs of those outside the church.

Especially to the Household of Faith

I hope we have seen here some of the concrete ways in which we can manifest the fruit of the Spirit in the life of the church. I hope we see that the fruit of the Spirit is not in any way a set of abstract morals but rather the concrete manifestation of the righteousness of Christ wrought by the Spirit in the day-in and day-out life of the church. That means that churches should faithfully support their pastors. It means that we should live desiring to shower our families, churches, and anyone we meet with the fruit of the Spirit. The bottom line is that the church should be a community marked by the love of Christ.

> Beloved, let us love one another, for love is from God, and whoever loves has been born of God and knows God. Anyone who does not love does not know God, because God is love. In this the love of God was made manifest among us, that God sent his only Son into the world, so that we might live through him. In this is love, not that we have loved God but that he loved us and sent his Son to be the propitiation for our sins. Beloved, if God so loved us, we also ought to love one another. (1 John 4:7–11)

Bearing the fruit of the Spirit is the very essence of what it means to be spiritual.

22

Peace Upon the Israel of God

GALATIANS 6:11–18

But far be it from me to boast except in the cross of our Lord Jesus Christ, by which the world has been crucified to me, and I to the world. For neither circumcision counts for anything, nor uncircumcision, but a new creation. And as for all who walk by this rule, peace and mercy be upon them, and upon the Israel of God. From now on let no one cause me trouble, for I bear on my body the marks of Jesus. The grace of our Lord Jesus Christ be with your spirit, brothers. Amen.

We at last come to the conclusion of Paul's letter to the Galatian churches. In this important letter, Paul has fought off the heretical beliefs of the false teachers, those who claimed that Gentiles had to believe in Jesus *and* be circumcised. Paul quickly called this a false gospel and warned the Galatians that anyone, man or angel, who preached a different gospel other than the one they heard from Paul and the apostles, would be condemned. Paul in fact repeated this warning twice (Gal. 1:8–9).

Throughout his epistle, Paul sets forth the doctrine of justification by faith alone—we are saved by grace alone through faith alone in Christ alone. The obedience, suffering, and resurrection of Christ saves us. Our faith is not introspective, but *extraspective*. We look to the work of another. At the same time, Christ's work constitutes the dawning of the new creation. The failed kingdom of Adam, now under the control of Satan, sin, and death, is coming to nothing, and the kingdom of Christ has dawned. Christ's kingdom, in total antithesis to the failed kingdom of Adam, is marked by righteousness and holiness. In a word, the outpouring of the Spirit produces righteous fruit. Paul has also shown how this fruit should be manifest in the life of the church and in individual believers. Because Christ has poured out the Spirit upon us, we should be marked by humility, in gently restoring the repentant sinner. We should see to the financial needs of the pastor, the one who preaches and teaches the Word. We should continue steadfastly in doing good. And, we should love all people, but especially the household of faith, the church.

Although Paul's letter is relatively short, it is nevertheless pregnant with incisive truth and application. And before Paul closes out his letter, he has several more important things to say. I think it is fair to say that Paul closes his letter with a bang! One might think that Paul is just saying farewell. Far from it, Paul essentially sums up the content of his letter in a few short verses.

In Whom Do We Boast?

At the beginning of this section, Paul concludes his letter as it was common for him to do. He took the pen from the scribe and wrote with large letters to emphasize the importance of his point (v. 11).[1] Paul states two of the chief motivating factors for the false teachers: "It is those who want to make a good showing in the flesh who would force you to be circumcised, and only in order that they may not be persecuted for the cross of Christ. For even those who are circumcised do not themselves keep the law, but they desire to have you circumcised that they may boast in your flesh" (Gal. 6:12–13). Paul points out that the first motivating factor behind the false teachers was the desire to avoid persecution.

The majority of first-century Jews saw Christianity as an aberration, a sect of Judaism. Like the pre-converted Paul, they persecuted the church for worshipping what they thought was a false Messiah and encouraging Gentiles who "converted" to forsake Israel's law, specifically circumcision. The false teachers, therefore, were encouraging the Gentiles to be circumcised, not only because they believed it was still necessary, but because they thought this would also spare them from persecution. They could point to the Gentile converts and say, "See! They are keeping the law. They submit to circumcision."

Second, they were prone to boasting, perhaps much like many pastors in our own day. Some pastors will boast, not in Christ, but in how big their churches are and how many people attend. We foster this type of mentality because we take far too many of our cues from the world rather than from Scripture. How does the world measure success? Bigger is always better, more is better than less, and some is better than none. Hence, a megachurch pastor that preaches to thousands each Sunday is better than the minister who preaches to mere hundreds. But what many fail to see is that the Scriptures do not measure success in terms of numbers but in terms of fidelity to God's call to preach the gospel. This is Paul's point in his criticism of the

---

1. Thomas Schreiner, *Galatians*, ZECNT (Grand Rapids, MI: Zondervan, 2010), 376.

false teachers. In Paul's day, the false teachers were boasting in their success with Gentile converts. They wanted people to see how many Gentiles they had been able to convince to submit to circumcision. Paul has identified and established these points in his epistle. But like a prizefighter that has pummeled his opponent, but saves enough energy for a series of knockout blows, Paul hits the false teachers with a powerful combination of punches to show how they have not been faithful to the gospel of Christ.

Marked by Christ

To see Paul's first punch we must note the contrast he has established. The false teachers wanted to have the Gentiles circumcised. As a result, they were also marked by boasting—boasting in their own accomplishments. By contrast, Paul had unique marks of his own: "I bear on my body the marks of Jesus" (Gal. 6:17). Paul was undoubtedly a scarred man—marked by scars from his 138 lashes, his near-fatal stoning, and his multiple shipwrecks (2 Cor. 11:16–29). Paul calls these scars the marks of Jesus. They were the marks that he bore as a result of being united to Christ—they were the shared sufferings of Christ. These were the marks by which Paul wanted to be associated and known, not circumcision. He did not want to be marked by the abrogated ceremonial law, but by Christ.

This is why Paul writes in verse 15: "For neither circumcision counts for anything, nor uncircumcision, but new creation" (Gal. 6:15*). Paul explains that circumcision matters not, but only "new creation." Paul does not say one must be a new creature; he does not imply that Christianity is a "fresh start." No, he invokes the ancient promises about the new heavens and earth from the prophet Isaiah: "For behold, I create new heavens and a new earth, and the former things shall not be remembered or come into mind" (Isa. 65:17). Indeed, in Christ, God had begun to create the new heavens and earth. Paul says, in effect: "You false teachers and your followers are marked by the old creation. I, Paul, on the other hand, only want to be marked by Christ. Mine are the marks of the new creation. Self-congratulatory boasting marks you; I only want to boast in the cross of Christ. Only Christ brings the promises of the new heavens and earth through his cross of reconciliation, through his life, death, resurrection, ascension, and the outpouring of the power of the age to come, the Holy Spirit."

The Israel of God

If his first punch left Paul's opponents reeling, then surely this second punch sent them to the mat for the final count. To understand its significance, we should first take a step back to the Old Testament, once again to the book of Isaiah. At the time, Israel was in exile for their sin—in his judgment God kicked Israel out of the Promised Land. This, however, was not the last word on the matter. God promised through the prophet that the exile would end; God would return his people to the Promised Land:

> "In overflowing anger for a moment I hid my face from you, but with everlasting love I will have compassion on you," says the LORD, your Redeemer. This is like the days of Noah to me: as I swore that the waters of Noah should no more go over the earth, so I have sworn that I will not be angry with you, and will not rebuke you. For the mountains may depart and the hills be removed, but my steadfast love shall not depart from you, and my covenant of peace shall not be removed," says the LORD, who has compassion on you. (Isaiah 54:8–10)

Isaiah employs new-creation language. The prophet describes their return from exile like the receding Noahic flood waters, which was a re-creation, or renewing of the creation. Within the greater context of the conclusion of Galatians, remember, Paul has just said that neither circumcision nor uncircumcision matters but only new creation counts for something. Verse 10 describes what God will do for Israel: "'For the mountains may depart and the hills be removed, but my steadfast love [*mercy*, LXX] shall not depart from you, and my covenant of *peace* shall not be removed,' says the LORD, who has compassion on you" (Isa. 54:10; emphasis added). The Lord says through the prophet to Israel that he will give them his "mercy" and "peace."[2]

Now, we can return to Galatians: "For neither circumcision counts for anything, nor uncircumcision, but new creation. And as for all who walk by this rule, peace and mercy be upon them, and upon the Israel of God" (Gal. 6:15–16*). Remember, if anyone is in Christ, he is a new creation. And, now, notice verse 16. This is stunning: anyone, Jew or Gentile, circumcised or not, if he is in Christ, belongs to Israel. The one who looks to Christ by faith is the Israel of God! Paul applies this title to uncircumcised Gentiles, which any ordinary Jew would think applied exclusively to circumcised Jews. The false teachers were trying too hard to be identified as Israel, because they thought the law and adherence to it is what made them unique, but Paul drops this bomb on them. Regardless of their efforts, only those who belong to Christ are properly called Israel. Paul had earlier made this point, when he wrote: "Know then that it is those of faith who are the sons of Abraham" (Gal. 3:7). Paul's argument is a stroke of genius, inspired at that; falsehood collapses in the face of the truth.

You Are the Israel of God!

Dear Christian, meditate upon your identity as the Israel of God. You were far off, aliens to the commonwealth of Israel, strang-

---

2. G. K. Beale, "Peace and Mercy Upon the Israel of God: The Old Testament Background in Galatians 6:16," *Biblica* 80 (1999): 204–223.

ers, but now you have been brought near and adopted as God's sons. You are Israel! Who broke down the wall of separation? Jesus Christ. Christ poured out his Holy Spirit upon us, raised us from death to life, replaced our heart of stone with one of flesh, gave us eyes to see and ears to hear, and engrafted us into Israel. Indeed, if Christ is the true Israel of God, then those who look to Christ by faith and are united to him become the Israel of God. We now share in all of the blessings promised to Israel because of Christ. Indeed, we are new creatures through Christ. If these things are true, then what does it say about the one in whom we boast?

Do we boast in ourselves? While boasting in the circumcision of our flesh is no longer a problem in the church, at the same time we have found other idols about which to boast, other reasons to put ourselves first. The world boasts in itself—at every turn the world creates a reason to put itself first and oftentimes we find such thinking influencing the conduct of the church. So often the "look-at-me" culture has infiltrated the church, from the pulpit to the pew. When the church becomes about what we want, about boasting in ourselves, it ceases to be about boasting in what Christ has done. The church cannot be about us. You have heard the saying from the cowboy movies of old, "This town ain't big enough for the both of us." The same holds true for the church. Christ is not into time-sharing. We either give him the sole place of honor and boast only in him, or we have no part in him. Paul's answer is clear: "But far be it from me to boast except in the cross of our Lord Jesus Christ, by which the world has been crucified to me, and I to the world" (Gal. 6:14).

AUTHOR

J. V. FESKO (Ph.D. Kings College, University of Aberdeen) is Academic Dean and Associate Professor of Systematic Theology and Historical Theology at Westminster Seminary California. Previously, Dr. Fesko served for ten years as pastor of Geneva Orthodox Presbyterian Church in Woodstock, Georgia.

SERIES EDITOR

JON D. PAYNE (M.Th. New College, University of Edinburgh; D.Min., Reformed Theological Seminary) has served as pastor of Grace Presbyterian Church (PCA) in Douglasville, Georgia since 2003. Dr. Payne is a Visiting Lecturer in Practical Theology at RTS Atlanta and the author of *In the Splendor of Holiness* and *John Owen on the Lord's Supper.*